The Modern Nations in

Historical Perspective

ROBIN W. WINKS, General Editor

The volumes in this series deal with individual
nations or groups of closely related nations
throughout the world, summarizing the chief historical trends and influences that have contributed
to each nation's present-day character, problems,
and behavior. Recent data are incorporated with
established historical background to achieve a
fresh synthesis and original interpretation.

The authors of this volume, CHARLES AND BARBARA
JELAVICH, are respectively Professor and Associate Professor in the History Department at Indiana University. Each has a large background of
study and travel in the Balkan States. Both have
written authoritative works on the Balkans, Russia, and Eastern Europe in general. Among Mr.
Jelavich's books is Tsarist Russia and Balkan Nationalism. Mrs. Jelavich is the author of Russia
and the Rumanian National Cause, 1858-1859
and A Century of Russian Foreign Policy. Together the Jelaviches have edited The Balkans in
Transition and The Education of a Russian Statesman: The Memoirs of Nicholas Karlovich Giers.

THE BALKANS

THE BALKANS AFTER 1945

THE BALKANS

Charles and Barbara Jelavich

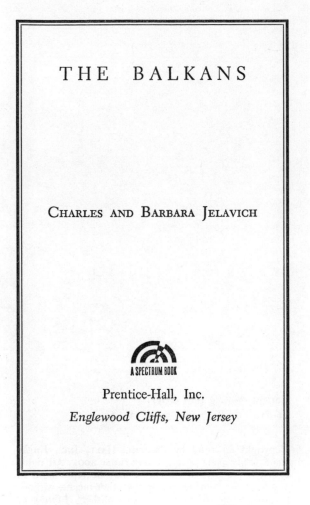

A SPECTRUM BOOK

Prentice-Hall, Inc.

Englewood Cliffs, New Jersey

This book concerns the history of five modern nations—Albania, Bulgaria, Greece, Rumania, and Yugoslavia—all located on the Balkan peninsula. The designation *Balkan* is and has been a matter of controversy. It is clear that Albania, Bulgaria, and Yugoslavia belong to this category, but the inclusion of Greece and Rumania is open to question. It can be argued that Rumania is tied more closely to the other Danubian states; Greece is perhaps best dealt with as an eastern Mediterranean country. The omission of Hungary and Turkey, both of which have played a major role in Balkan history and hold or have held extensive territory in the Balkans, can also be criticized. The choice of the five states included is based on the geographic unity of the peninsula and on modern conditions. It is, however, strongly recommended that the reader study, in connection with this survey, two associated volumes: *Austria and Hungary*, by R. John Rath, and *Turkey*, by Roderic H. Davison, to obtain a better understanding of the entire general area.

In the narrative the emphasis has been placed on those aspects of the past which, the authors believe, contribute to an understanding of the present. Therefore, the main topic throughout has been Balkan nationalism and the development of each state as a political unit. There is less emphasis on the medieval period and on certain economic, social, political, and diplomatic problems, which—while predominant in their own epoch—have lost much of their significance today.

Books in English on more specialized subjects and national histories have been given in the section *Suggested Readings*. This is a selective list,

vii

not a complete one. It will be noted that some subjects, in particular the diplomatic history of the Eastern Question in the nineteenth century, have received intensive study; others, notably domestic issues within the Balkan states, have been given much less attention. In the same manner current politics have aroused much interest in contrast to the period between the wars, which has been largely neglected. For further information on Balkan history, the reader is strongly advised to refer to Leften S. Stavrianos, *The Balkans Since 1453* (New York: Holt, Rinehart & Winston, Inc., 1958) and the essays in Charles and Barbara Jelavich (eds.), *The Balkans in Transition* (Berkeley: University of California Press, 1963). The authors have made extensive use of both books in the preparation of this volume.

The multiplicity of languages in the Balkans presents some difficulties in regard to the spelling of names of places and people. In general, the form used generally in books in English has been adopted. Where possible this spelling is that used in the nation or by the person concerned. The transliteration of Serbian, Bulgarian, and Greek names has been, in general, in accordance with the Library of Congress system.

The authors would like to express their gratitude to Professors Ivo Lederer and Wayne Vucinich of Stanford University, and to Professor Nicolas Spulber of Indiana University, who read and commented upon the manuscript. They also wish to thank Professor Robin Winks of Yale University, the editor of this series, and Mr. William Green of Prentice-Hall, Inc. for their valuable advice and assistance in editorial matters. As always, Mark and Peter Jelavich have also contributed greatly to the preparation of this book.

C.J.
B.J.

CONTENTS

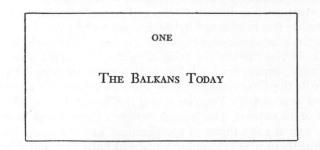

ONE

THE BALKANS TODAY

Albania, Bulgaria, Greece, Rumania, and Yugoslavia cover approximately 295,000 square miles (an area somewhat larger than Texas), and contain a population of more than 56 million. The Balkan lands have earned an unenviable reputation in modern times; indeed the very word *Balkan* is associated with violence, disorder, and recurring warfare. The expression *Balkanization*, when applied to other areas, refers to an undesirable political fragmentation; the phrase *Balkan politics* is used to describe frequent and haphazard changes of government and general corruption. These characteristics of injustice and violence are reflected in the literature of the best of the Balkan writers, notably Ivo Andrić and Nikos Kazantzakis.

In contrast to this dark picture, the Balkans have frequently been the setting for comic operas and romantic tales of improbable kingdoms and heroic adventures. Montenegro is the scene of Franz Lehár's *The Merry Widow*; the Serbo-Bulgarian War of 1885 is the central event in G. B. Shaw's *Arms and the Man*, which was subsequently made into the operetta, *The Chocolate Soldier*. The Balkans also have provided the background for innumerable stories of espionage, intrigue, and adventure, and one of the best accounts of the supernatural, *Dracula*.

In international relations, the Balkan peninsula has acquired the reputation of being a "tinderbox," the "powderkeg of Europe." This description was certainly accurate in the nineteenth century, when European diplomacy was dominated by the so-called Eastern Question, which concerned the breakup of the Ottoman Empire. In a period characterized by general tranquillity in the rest of Europe, the Balkan peninsula was the scene of conflicts in 1821-29, 1853-56, 1877-78, 1897, and 1912-13. The incident which led to World War I occurred in Bosnia. In addition, there were constant uprisings in certain areas, such as Bosnia, Crete, and Macedonia. The appearance of instability was heightened by the frequent and violent *coups d'état* in both the nineteenth and twentieth centuries. Political change and unrest have also marked the years after the two world wars. Greece, for example, experienced a bitter civil war in 1947-49. Yugoslavia's break with the Communist bloc in 1949 and Albania's championing of China against both Yugoslavia and the Soviet Union affected the policies of all nations. The tension between Greece and Turkey over Cyprus, carrying the threat of open conflict in the eastern Mediterranean, directly involved the military plans of both East and West.

In the following pages an attempt will be made to describe the conditions that led to these events and gained for the Balkans their sad reputation. For it must be admitted that the Balkan peninsula is indeed a land of conflict and contrast, of instability and change. Divided into five states, the Balkan peoples speak six languages: Albanian, Bulgarian, Greek, Rumanian, Serbo-Croatian, and Slovenian. This number may be increased to seven if Macedonian, which is very close to Bulgarian, is counted as a separate language. In addition, there are minorities speaking German, Italian, Magyar, and Turkish. The three major churches are the Catholic, the Moslem, and the Orthodox; there are Jewish and Protestant minorities. This condition of division and disunity is also apparent in international relations. Among the five Balkan states can be found representatives of the major political blocs; Albania now is joined with China; Bulgaria is part of the Soviet bloc; Greece is allied with the West; Yugoslavia is attempting to form a neutralist coalition; Rumania, although still formally tied to the Soviet bloc, is attempting to assert her independence, particularly in economic matters.

The Influence of Geography on Balkan Life

The first and perhaps the major cause for this diversity is the geography of the Balkan peninsula—the configuration of the land and its position in relation to that of other nations. The peninsula is a crossroads between Europe, Asia, and Africa. Here the peoples and cultures of three continents have met and mingled, or clashed and conquered. The major powers of each historical epoch have made their influence felt here and have left their mark upon the peoples. The great imperial powers of the past—Greeks, Romans, Turks, Venetians, Austrians, Germans, French, British, and Russians—all in their turn have dominated or sought to dominate the area.

The establishment of foreign influence, made possible by the accessibility of the peninsula to the three continents, has been facilitated by the terrain itself. *Balkan* is the Turkish word for *mountain*, and it is this aspect of the landscape that has most clearly shaped the political destiny of its people. The great mountain chains of the peninsula—the Carpathians in Rumania, the Balkan and Rhodope mountains in Bulgaria, the Dinaric Alps in Yugoslavia and Albania, and the Pindus range in Greece—have effectively isolated the different peoples from one another and have contributed to a fragmentation of political power. Lacking a geographic center, the peninsula became divided into a number of small states which were generally in conflict with one another.

Although the shape of the land encouraged political divisions among the people, it also allowed easy penetration by foreign armies. The peninsula is cut by the great natural highways formed by the rivers and the mountains. Three of these routes are of particular importance in the history of the Balkans. The first runs along the north shore of the Black Sea through Rumania, then along the Danube River into central Europe. Historically, this was the gateway into the Balkans for the Asiatic tribes that influenced European, as well as Balkan, history. This road also branched southward, through Bulgaria, to the imperial city of Constantinople (now Istanbul). This was the route used in the many Russian campaigns against the Ottoman Empire in the eighteenth and nineteenth centuries. The second highway runs along the Danube from Vienna to Belgrade and Niš, where it divides: one branch continues along the Vardar River to the port of Thessaloniki; the other leads through Sofia, along the Maritsa River, to Constantinople. The third route, chiefly important in ancient times, is the Via Egnatia, which was the main route between Rome and her eastern provinces. It passes through Albania and northern Greece and goes on to Constantinople. These roads, relatively free of natural obstacles, opened the peninsula to foreign conquest, making it a battleground for the armies of three continents.

The Balkans were open not only from the land, but also from the sea. Surrounded by the Adriatic, the Aegean, and the Black Sea, the coastal areas still bear the marks of conquest left by the great sea powers of the past. For example, Venice held Crete, Dalmatia, and the Morea (the Peloponnesus) for long periods; Britain dominated the waters of the eastern Mediterranean in the nineteenth century. Greece, the only Balkan maritime nation, exerted influence on the Rumanian and Bulgarian coastal regions.

Because of the accessibility of the peninsula by both land and sea, and because of its immense strategic importance, the area has enjoyed only short periods of political independence since the middle of the fourteenth century. The most important influence was the almost five hundred years of Ottoman domination over at least some portion of the Balkans. Although most of the Balkan peoples escaped Turkish rule during the nineteenth century, the states then established usually fell under the direct domination of a stronger power or were part of the sphere of influence of another state. Divided among themselves and economically backward, the Balkans have enjoyed a brief and precarious independence only when their great neighbors were in a state of political balance. At other times, they have fallen under the influence of the strongest military power on the continent. After World War I, for example, the Balkans came under the influence of France and then of Germany. After World War II the Soviet Union was able to determine the political structure and foreign policy of most of the Balkan governments. The policies initiated by the United States under the Truman Doctrine of 1947 improved the political balance of the Balkans and allowed individual states more freedom of movement. Nevertheless, it must be remembered that the Balkan peninsula has been and, to a degree, is still a dependent area. The freedom of action—indeed, the economic well-being—of the individual states depends largely on the great powers and general world politics rather than on the decisions arrived at in the Balkan capitals.

The Balkan States in the Modern World

ALBANIA. The poorest and least known of the Balkan countries, Albania did not become an independent state until just before World War I. Thereafter much of her energy was devoted to preserving herself from partition by her neighbors. The most ancient of the peoples of the peninsula, the Albanians speak a Thraco-Illyrian language unrelated to those of their neighbors. The state, about the size of Maryland, covers approximately 12,000 square miles. The population of the country is about 1.7 million, but another 750,000 Albanians live outside the national confines—the largest group in the adjacent Kosovo-Mctohija (Kosmct) district of Yugoslavia. Of particular interest is the fact that 70 per cent of the population is Moslem, a condition unique in Europe. During the Turkish occupation only this area and Bosnia, along with parts of Macedonia, saw mass conversions to Islam. Of the remaining population, about 20 per cent are Orthodox and 10 per cent are Catholic. The people are further divided into two groups. The Ghegs inhabit the mountains and live in extremely primitive conditions; the Tosks control the best lands near the coast and have always had the advantage of closer relations with the outside world (with the Greeks and Italians in particular). The Tosks have also emigrated and large Tosk communities exist in Italy and in the United States.

The most economically backward of the Balkan peoples, the Albanians also have the highest birth and death rates in eastern Europe. The land itself offers little promise of a more prosperous future. Only 16 per cent of it is arable and, although vast forests exist, they cannot be readily exploited. The mineral wealth of the country had been largely undeveloped, although oil and chrome ore are now exported. Communications are very poor; the first standard-gauge railroads were not completed until after World War II. Most of the existing roads were constructed by the Italians during their periods of occupation. The only good port, Durazzo (Durres), has been coveted by both Italy and Yugoslavia because of its importance for Adriatic trade.

The present government was set up after World War II, when the Communist-led partisan movement of Enver Hoxha gained military control of the country. Postwar Albania's close association with Yugoslavia ended when Belgrade and Moscow broke their political ties in 1948. After that, the Albanian government followed the political direction of the Soviet Union and leaned heavily upon that state for economic support. Like the other socialist countries, Albania attempted to build up her industry and collectivized her agriculture. In 1960, however, the antagonism which had been developing between China and the Soviet Union was brought into the open. Albania, alone among the European socialist states, chose to support China. This position was primarily influenced by her rift with Yugoslavia and the latter's improved relations with the Soviet Union after 1956. Thus Albania now stands alone, without European allies. Her political doctrines divide her from the West; her relations with her southern neighbor, Greece, are embittered by Greek claims on parts of Albania. Although some ties with Italy have been renewed, Albanian memories of past Italian domination prevent too close an association. China, because of her own economic weakness and her great distance, can be of little assistance. Despite this condition, Albania's political alignment and her refusal to follow in the path of the other socialist states of Europe has enabled her to play a role in international affairs far outweighing her actual strength.

BULGARIA. In contrast to Albania, Bulgaria has maintained her close adherence to the Soviet bloc established after World War II. Of all the nations of eastern Europe, it is Bulgaria whose relations with the Soviet Union are the best and have the strongest historical basis for existence. Both the Bulgarians and the Russians are Slavs; their languages are the most closely related within the Slavic group. Both are predominantly Orthodox in religion. In the nineteenth century Russian support enabled Bulgaria to gain her independence and, despite frequent disagreements between the governments, the Russians have probably enjoyed more popularity among the Bulgarians than among any other people.

Of the Balkan states, Bulgaria has had the most consistently unsuccessful foreign policy. In three wars—1913, 1914-18, and 1939-45 —she supported the losing side. As a consequence, Bulgaria, like Albania, benefited less from the partition of the former Ottoman Empire than did those of her neighbors who pursued more fortunate courses of action.

The present boundaries of Bulgaria enclose an area of about 43,000 square miles (the size of the state of Tennessee) and hold a population of some 8 million. Like her neighbors, Bulgaria is not a rich land; only about 38 per cent of the territory is arable. Until recently, few attempts have been made to discover and exploit the mineral resources in the mountain areas. Before World War II, the country was primarily a land of small, peasant holdings worked by traditional methods. In 1945, Bulgaria, like the other states of eastern and central Europe, adopted a political and economic system patterned after that of the Soviet Union. Following in the path of the other Soviet-bloc countries, she embarked upon a program of rapid industrialization. Particular attention has been paid to the development of heavy industry and an entirely new iron and steel complex has been built up. As in other socialist countries, however, real advances in industry have been balanced by failures in agriculture. After the war, a policy of collectivization and mechanization was introduced, but with little success. Production has not been adequate and shortages have developed repeatedly.

At present, Bulgaria remains closely linked with the Soviet Union. Her press and radio reflect, more exactly than do those of her neighbors, the opinions of Moscow. Her policy of close cooperation with the Soviet Union has brought her into conflict with Yugoslavia, Greece, and Turkey, all of which belong to other international alignments. The Macedonian question—involving Bulgarian claims on lands now held by Greece and Yugoslavia—and Bulgaria's desire for an outlet on the Aegean have also served to embitter her relations with her neighbors. Her relations with Rumania, despite the fact that both states are a part of the Soviet bloc, have been subject to strain. In the past, the chief point of dispute between Rumania and Bulgaria has been the possession of southern Dobrudja, which has changed hands three times in half a century.

RUMANIA. In contrast to Bulgaria, Rumania, the second Balkan state to establish close relations with the Soviet bloc, has a tradition of opposition to the Russians and to the Slavic states as a whole. The Rumanians are able to trace their national ancestry to an ancient civilization, the Roman Empire—a link reflected in the Rumanian language, which is based on Latin. In the modern period, much influence has been exerted in the region by Greece and also by France. Although in many respects Rumania is unique among the Balkan states, her history and geographic position associate her closely with the area.

The modern Rumanian state—which now covers an area of about 91,000 square miles, or slightly less than that of Oregon—was formed by the union of three distinct areas: the two Danubian Principalities (Moldavia and Wallachia) and Transylvania, a former Habsburg possession. The complete unification of the state was not accomplished until after World War I. Wallachia and Moldavia were never fully subjected to Ottoman rule and their autonomy was reconfirmed in 1829. In 1861 the two provinces united to form Rumania. The third area, Transylvania, was closely associated with Hungary throughout most of its history and even today has a substantial Magyar minority. Of Rumania's 18.5 million inhabitants, about 1.5 million are Magyars and 350,000 are Germans. Approximately 80 per cent of the population is Orthodox.

Despite Rumania's ties with western Europe, her political fate has always been largely dependent upon Russia. The conflicts between Russia and the Ottoman Empire often made it necessary for Russian armies to march through Rumania, although usually as friends and allies. Rumania, like Bulgaria, was an active military ally of Germany in World War II. Rumanian soldiers took a prominent part in the German campaigns in the Soviet Union. The defeat of Germany naturally resulted in a Soviet military occupation of Rumania. Under the guise of war reparations, the Soviet authorities removed from the country a great deal of equipment—perhaps as much as $2 billion worth. They also supervised the establishment of a Communist regime. Because the Communist party in Rumania was very weak, and because Rumania (unlike Bulgaria) had no great tradition of friendship to Russia, severe measures of control were necessary.

Postwar Rumania followed the political and economic pattern of the socialist-bloc states, with the concentration on the development of industry and with the collectivization of agriculture. The Soviet Union had taken much from the country, but it was now forced to return a great deal in the form of credits and needed supplies. Close association with Moscow was, however, never extremely popular. By 1963 signs of resentment of Soviet control had become increasingly apparent and Rumania initiated efforts to re-establish a more independent position in international affairs.

Like the other Balkan states, Rumania has territorial disputes with her neighbors. The chief point of conflict has been with Russia over Bessarabia. This province, the inhabitants of which are predominantly Rumanian, was taken by Russia from the Ottoman Empire in 1812. In 1856 it was transferred to Moldavia, but Russia again acquired it in 1878. After World War I Rumanian possession was established once more, but during World War II it was incorporated into the Soviet Union as the Moldavian Socialist Republic. At that time the Soviet Union also annexed northern and central Bukovina, which had belonged to Rumania since 1918, and which had a large Ruthenian population. Rumania's annexation of Transylvania in 1919 naturally has led to disputes with Hungary, which refused to recognize the legitimacy of the transfer. Quarrels have also arisen over the Rumanian treatment of the Hungarian minority in Transylvania. Similarly, Rumania's acquisition of those portions of the Banat which border on Yugoslavia have led to disputes with that country. The province of Dobrudja has always been a point of conflict between Rumania and Bulgaria.

Despite her past difficulties, Rumania has enormous possibilities for future development. The lands of the Danubian plain have always returned rich harvests; at Ploesti can be found oil deposits which in Europe rank only after those of Baku in the Soviet Union. The Carpathian mountains have not only great timber resources, but also stores of gold, silver, lead, and zinc.

YUGOSLAVIA. Although Albania does not cooperate with Bulgaria and Rumania in international relations, all three countries depend upon another major power. Yugoslavia, in contrast, has tried to follow a policy of nonalignment and to benefit from the conflict between East and West. Today Yugoslavia covers approximately 98,000 square miles (the area of Wyoming), and has a population of some 19 million. During World War II the Communist-dominated partisan movement, under the leadership of Josip Broz Tito, gained both military and political control of the country. Thus Yugoslavia's postwar socialist regime, unlike those of Bulgaria and Rumania, came about because of domestic developments and with little Soviet assistance. Nevertheless, during its first years the new regime cooperated with the Soviet Union and its internal affairs followed the pattern of the other socialist states. By 1948-49, however, sharp disagreements between Yugoslavia and the Soviet Union led to the ultimate defection of Belgrade from the Soviet camp. The government also made changes in the political and economic system and in 1953 abandoned the attempt to collectivize agriculture. Although Yugoslavia's relations with the Soviet Union have improved, she has not returned to membership in the Soviet bloc. Instead, she has attempted to join with the nonaligned nations, such as Egypt and India, to form a third camp in international politics.

Yugoslavia today is a federation of six republics, the boundaries of which coincide roughly with the historical divisions of the state. The country is perhaps the most interesting in the Balkans because of its diversity. Although all the people, except for the minorities which are found in all Balkan lands, are South Slavs and have related languages, they differ widely in many other respects. Two distinct languages, Serbo-Croatian and Slovenian, are spoken; if Macedonia is considered as a separate language, the number rises to three. The country has three major religions. Of the 86 per cent of the population who reported their faith in 1953, 42 per cent were Orthodox, 32 per cent Catholic, and 12 per cent Moselm. Moreover, the political subdivisions have preserved their identities and unique characteristics. A brief survey of these regions is essential for an understanding of modern Yugoslavia, for the history of the entire area has been largely that of the development of these sections. The chief internal problem of the state of Yugoslavia, which came into existence only in 1918, has been that of governing and attempting to develop a national consciousness among peoples with different historical experiences and at various economic levels.

The area lying furthest to the north, Slovenia, has enjoyed perhaps the most fortunate history of any Balkan land. Joined early in its development to the Habsburg Empire, it did not suffer the frequent wars that devastated the other territories. Largely owing to this circumstance, Slovenia has been and remains the most prosperous of the Yugoslav lands. Its language, Slovenian, is not easily intelligible to the rest of the population. The predominant religion is Catholicism and the general pattern of life resembles that of the other peoples who once formed a part of the Habsburg Empire.

Croatia, like Slovenia, was long associated with the Habsburg Empire. Croatia, however, had once been an independent kingdom and always preserved a degree of autonomy, even under foreign rule. Highly conscious of their own identity, the Croats have always resisted centralizing tendencies, whether these emanated from Vienna or from Belgrade. The predominant religion in Croatia is Catholicism; the language, although essentially identical to that spoken in Serbia, is written in the Latin alphabet rather than the Cyrillic.

Croatia also includes the historic provinces of Slavonia and Dalmatia. Separated from Bosnia by the rugged Dinaric Alps, Dalmatia has a unique history. Here the imprint of the Venetian conquest and of Italian influence can be seen. One of its cities, Dubrovnik, was second only to Venice in commerical importance on the Adriatic from the fourteenth to the seventeenth centuries. Today, Dubrovnik is one of the best preserved of the medieval cities of Europe. The people of Dalmatia are predominantly Croatian and Catholic.

The province of Bosnia-Hercegovina marks the dividing line between Serbs and Croats, Orthodoxy and Catholicism. It also has a high proportion (30 per cent) of Moslems, for this area, like Albania, had many conversions during the Ottoman occupation. One of the most backward of the Yugoslav republics, Bosnia was freed from Ottoman control only in 1878. Its capital, Sarajevo, was the site of the incident that started World War I.

The most successful independent national history belongs to Serbia. The strongest of the federal republics of present-day Yugoslavia, it contains more than 40 per cent of the population of the country. Its major city, Belgrade, is the capital of Yugoslavia and its administrative center. Serbia's dominant religion is Orthodoxy. The language is written in the Cyrillic alphabet. The general pattern of life is similar to that in lands that formed part of the Ottoman Empire, rather than those which were once under Habsburg rule. Within Serbia itself there are two autonomous areas, Kosovo-Metohija (Kosmet), with its Albanian population, and the Vojvodina, which has a large Hungarian minority.

The fifth section, Montenegro, has had perhaps the most romantic national history. This extremely primitive and mountainous region was able to maintain its independence when the rest of the peninsula fell under Ottoman control. Essentially Serbian and Orthodox, it differs little from neighboring Serbia.

The last, Macedonia, is the most controversial of the republics. Macedonia has throughout its history been fought over by Bulgarians, Greeks, Serbs, and Albanians, all of whom have claims on her territory. The province was not freed from Turkish control until 1912, and it his remained the most backward part of Yugoslavia. At present, the area has its own political organization and Macedonian is recognized as a distinct language.

The joining together of these sections into one state in 1918 posed difficult problems for the central government. Although the situation was somewhat alleviated by the creation of the six republics, the predominant position of Serbia in Yugoslavia still arouses much ill feeling in the other areas. The present regime has also made a great effort to build up the underdeveloped regions of Bosnia-Hercegovina, Macedonia, and Montenegro. Because this development must be carried out at the expense of the richer sections, such as Slovenia, much opposition has been aroused. Although Yugoslavia, like Rumania, has great economic potentialities, much needs to be done to realize them.

Like the other Balkan states, Yugoslavia has had disputes with all her neighbors. The question of the boundary with Italy—in particular, the fate of Trieste—has caused continual friction with Rome.

Similar territorial disagreements exist with Austria, Hungary, and Rumania. The dispute over Macedonia continues to influence Yugoslav relations with Bulgaria and Greece. The Kosmet area, with its overwhelmingly Albanian population, is a point of conflict with Albania.

GREECE. The fifth independent Balkan state, Greece, is the only one that has kept its prewar political form. It is today a constitutional monarchy with a multiparty system and a free economy. Covering about 51,000 square miles, it is approximately the size of Alabama. The Balkan character of Greece, like that Rumania, has been a matter of dispute. Although Macedonia is characteristically Balkan, the history of most of Greece has been more closely associated with that of the Mediterranean countries.

Today, Greece has a rapidly increasing population, currently some 8.5 million. It is Orthodox in religion and, since the population exchanges with Turkey in the 1920s, has no large minorities within its borders. The capital of the country is Athens, which, with the port of Piraeus, has about a million inhabitants. Modern Greek is related to the ancient language and the people pride themselves on their relationship to the great civilization of antiquity. The country is, however, faced with grave internal difficulties. About two thirds of Greece is covered by mountains; only 25 per cent of the land is arable. As a result, Greece is forced to import about half of her food supplies. Because her industrial development is low, manufactured goods must also be imported. To pay for these imports, Greece exports tobacco, raisins, wine, olive oil, and fresh fruits. She also earns money from the tourist trade, from her merchant fleet, and from remittances sent by Greek emigrants and workers abroad. All these sources of income are closely tied to world conditions and subject to fluctuation. Postwar efforts to increase Greek agricultural and industrial production have not solved the problem. Since World War II, Greece has placed great reliance on foreign (chiefly American) economic and military aid. She has also become an associate member of the European Common Market.

Because of her strategic position, Greece has always been of great importance, particularly to Great Britain and France. During most of the nineteenth century, Britain was the dominant naval power in the eastern Mediterranean and thus exerted much influence in Athens. In 1947 Britain relinquished her commitments in the area to the United States. At that time the Greek government was faced with a

Communist-led rebellion, which was receiving aid from Albania, Bulgaria, and Yugoslavia. To prevent the last Balkan state from falling into the Soviet camp, the United States, through the Truman Doctrine, came to the support of both Greece and Turkey. Thereafter immense amounts of economic and military aid were poured into Greece. In 1951 Greece and Turkey joined the North Atlantic Treaty Organization, and in 1953 both countries signed a mutual defense pact with Yugoslavia.

Greece, in international relations, is thus aligned with the West. A weakness of the Mediterranean defense system, however, is that much depends on cooperation between Greece and Turkey, two states with a long tradition of mutual hostility. Although an exchange of populations was carried out in the 1920s, there is a Turkish minority still in Thrace, and approximately 80,000 Greeks live in Istanbul (Constantinople). Since World War II, the chief dispute between the two nations has involved the fate of the island of Cyprus, where the Greeks outnumber the Turks by four to one. Greece also has territorial disputes with Albania, Bulgaria, and Yugoslavia.

Common Characteristics of the Balkan States

Although this brief survey has emphasized the differences within and among the Balkan states, many points of unity and similarity do exist. First in importance perhaps is the fact that the populations of all the Balkan states are predominantly of the peasant class. Even in Greece more than 50 per cent of the people still depend on the land for their livelihood. Furthermore, all the Balkan states lag behind the nations of central and western Europe in general economic development and have much lower standards of living. Nevertheless, every Balkan country, whether socialist or capitalist, is making an immense effort to alter this situation. The attempt is being made throughout the Balkans to transform backward peasant societies and economies into something more closely resembling those of the modern industrial states. Yet each country is also suffering from the effects of such rapid change.

In their efforts at modernization, the Balkan countries, like the Soviet Union, have taken the industrial civilizations of America and western Europe as their models. Therefore, the objects of daily life and the architecture of each country are fast losing their unique national qualities. The articles for sale at any large store in any of the Balkan countries reveal a depressing uniformity; the same great square grey apartment houses are replacing everywhere the really beautiful native architecture. This development, arising from social and economic necessity, has meant that the outward aspects of Balkan daily life are becoming increasingly similar to those of the rest of the Western world. The peasant woman of the Balkan village now buys dresses, made in the factories of her own country, very similar to those of the housewife of the American Midwest; the pots and pans in her kitchen may have been manufactured in state-owned plants which copied German designs. The unique and individual in each country is thus sacrificed in the interest of a developing industrial civilization and in the hope that a general improvement of living conditions will result.

The Balkan states share another quality: a history of foreign domination. In the past, as has been mentioned, the Balkan peoples have usually been under the control of other powers; this condition has lasted until the present. None of the Balkan states today, individually or with others, is capable of producing the complicated and extremely expensive weapons of the Atomic Age. The Balkan armies, a force to be reckoned with before World War II, have now lost much of their military value. Thus each of the Balkan states must rely on the patronage and protection of one of the great powers or depend on the maintenance of the balance of power between them. Under the circumstances, the principal concern of each Balkan government must naturally be its relations with the great powers and not its ties with its neighbors. Thus the hard realities of the international situation serve to make more difficult the relations among the Balkan nations and to intensify traditional rivalries.

In the following pages a short history of the development of the Balkan peoples and an explanation of the steps by which the modern Balkan states evolved will be given. The deep involvement of the United States government after World War II in this area, through its assistance to Greece and later Yugoslavia, brought it into a region where it had previously played only an insignificant role. It thus met directly and for the first time the multitude of problems which had occupied European diplomacy over the centuries.

TWO

THE MIDDLE AGES:

THE FORMATION OF BALKAN NATIONALITY

The basis of the five nations of the Balkan peninsula to-day was set by the end of the Middle Ages. This period is also of immense significance because at its close most of the peninsula fell under foreign rule for almost five centuries. The independent national life of the Balkan people thus came to a sudden close at the end of the fifteenth century. When the national liberation movements of the nineteenth and twentieth centuries took place, each of the Balkan nations looked back to the medieval period to secure strength for its own revival and to justify its claims to certain territories. The ancestors of the Albanians, the Greeks, and the Rumanians settled in the region in ancient times; the Slavic peoples of both Yugoslavia and Bulgaria appeared on the peninsula in the sixth century.

THE GREEKS. Among the Balkan peoples, it is undoubtedly the Greeks who have the longest and most illustrious national tradition. The civilization of ancient Greece forms the basis of Western culture. Although the actual composition of the Greek population has been much modified since ancient times, notably by the Slavic migrations of the seventh and eighth centuries and by Albanian and Turkish immigration, the Greek of today does indeed feel that he is the descendant of the ancient Greek and that his nation, alone among those of the Western world, has enjoyed an uninterrupted historical and cultural tradition of two thousand years' duration. This convic-

15

tion of a superior heritage has strongly influenced Greek policy and the relations of the Greeks with their neighbors.

Unlike the other Balkan countries, Greek life has always centered about the sea. The poverty of the Greek soil and the difficulty of internal communications have traditionally led the more enterprising Greeks to go abroad. In ancient times Greek traders and settlers found their way around the shores of the Mediterranean and into the Black Sea. In each epoch of Greek history it is the eastern Mediterranean, rather than the mainland, which has formed the core of Greek life.

The first great phase of Greek history is the ancient period. The cultural contributions of Athens, Sparta, Corinth, and Thebes are among the highest of the ancient world. The Greek city-states, however, fell before the attack of the Macedonian armies. Their great leader, Alexander the Great, during his brief reign (between 336 and 323 B.C.) led his troops as far as Afghanistan and India, a truly immense achievement for the age. Although Alexander's empire disintegrated upon his death, the Macedonian conquests extended Greek civilization and Greek supremacy into the Eastern world. Whereas Greece itself fell under Roman domination by the second century B.C., Greek culture and education maintained their unique position.

The center of Greek influence thereafter shifted from the mainland to the city of Constantinople. This imperial city, built by the Greeks and first named Byzantium, became the capital of the Roman Empire in A.D. 326, when Emperor Constantine made it his place of residence and gave it his name. At the end of the fourth century, when the Roman Empire in the West entered upon a period of full decline, Constantinople became the center of another Hellenic civilization. Although the empire over which it presided was Graeco-Roman in tradition, it was the Greek and not the Latin language that prevailed. The Byzantine Empire, which endured for more than a thousand years, is one of the most splendid of all world civilizations. The nature of this state and its traditions have exerted an enormous influence not only upon the Balkans, but also upon Russia.

The Byzantine state was of great significance for subsequent Balkan development because of its absolutist political system and its ecclesiastical organization. The Greek city-states had given to the West a liberal tradition. Greek Byzantium followed a different path: the political pattern transmitted by the Byzantine Empire to Russia and the Balkans was one of autocratic rule and a disenfranchised citizenry. It was this ideal of the autocrat that the princes of Moscow and the rulers of the Balkan states adopted as their own.

Equally important for the development of the Balkan nations were the relations of church and state within the Byzantine Empire. Here the emperor was able to impose his authority on the religious community. Because of this, parallels to the prolonged church-state disputes of western Europe are relatively rare in Byzantine history. The Christian church in the East supported and strengthened the political authority, but remained subordinate to it. This amalgamation of religious and political institutions was carried into the period of the Ottoman conquest, when the church became the state for the Balkan Christians.

From Constantinople, the Christian church also carried on the conversion of the Slavic peoples. Of particular importance were the activities of two brothers, Cyril and Methodius, who converted the Bulgarians. By the end of the tenth century Kievan Russia had also received Christianity through Byzantium. In 1054 the churches of Rome and Constantinople broke apart, never again to be united. The line of division between Eastern and Western Christianity ran directly through the Balkans. It followed in general the boundary between the former Eastern and Western Roman Empires. The people who lived in the west remained with the Church of Rome and were now called Catholics. They kept their patterns of Western civilization and culture. Those who lived in the eastern portion were under the jurisdiction of the Church of Constantinople and were henceforth known as Orthodox. Their civilization and their way of life were deeply influenced by Byzantium. They also later became more firmly subjected to Ottoman domination. In this division of the Balkans, which was to have deep and lasting effects, the Croats and the Slovenes became Catholics; the Albanians, the Bulgarians, the Greeks, the Macedonians, the Montenegrins, the Rumanians, and the Serbs were Orthodox.

THE RUMANIANS. The second nation with roots in the ancient world is Rumania—although, unlike Greece, it does not have a medieval tradition of similar importance. The origin of the first inhabitants of the present territory of Rumania is not known. The land, formerly known as Dacia, was conquered by Emperor Trajan in A.D. 106. During the period of Roman occupation, colonists were brought from other parts of the Roman Empire. By 275, however, pressure from the barbarian tribes forced the Romans to withdraw. They left behind the legacy of the name of the future state of Rumania and the basis for the Rumanian language.

The geographic position of these lands explains their subsequent miserable history. With no natural barriers to invasion from the east or the south, the greater and richer part of the territory lay open to incursions from barbarian tribes. For a thousand years after the Roman occupation, the area constituted a highway into Europe for a series of eastern invaders. The Avars, the Bulgarians, the Hungarians (Magyars), the Kumans, and the Tartars succeeded one another. It is believed that the native population, faced with annihilation, fled into the Carpathian mountains. Only at the end of the thirteenth century did settlements once again appear on the plain. Thereafter, the Rumanian-speaking population was divided into three political centers. The two most important were the provinces of Moldavia and Wallachia. These states were able to maintain at least a degree of autonomy until they were finally united in 1859-61 to form the modern Rumania. The third area, Transylvania, soon fell under the control of Hungary and remained under its jurisdiction until 1918. At the end of the sixteenth century, a Rumanian ruler, Michael the Brave of Wallachia, built a short-lived empire whose territories included, in general, those of modern Rumania. With this exception, the Rumanian people remained divided until after World War I.

THE SOUTH SLAVS. The largest group of Balkan peoples, the South Slavs, did not appear on the peninsula until the sixth century. An extremely primitive people with no connections with ancient civilizations, moved southward from their homeland (somewhere in what is now southwestern Russia) in individual tribes and clans led by their various chiefs. The geography of the Balkans contributed to the failure of these people to unite in a single political unit. Instead, they became and remained organized in the separate groups whose names are now reflected in the titles of the six constituent republics of Yugoslavia and of Bulgaria. In time, the Serbs moved into the present territories of Serbia, Bosnia, Hercegovina, and Montenegro, with representative groups also in Macedonia and Dalmatia. The Croats settled in Croatia, Slavonia, and Dalmatia; the Slovenes inhabited Carinthia, Carniola, and Istria. A large Slavic group also migrated to Bulgaria. The subsequent history of the South Slavs centers about the development of four centers: Bulgaria, Serbia, Croatia, and Slovenia.

THE BULGARIANS. The word *Bulgarian* derives, not from the Slavic settlers, but from a tribe of Finno-Tatar invaders who subjugated the Slavic inhabitants in the seventh century and were later Slavicized by their subjects. In the ninth century the Bulgarians were converted to Christianity by the missionary activities of Cyril and Methodius, "the apostles of the Slavs." The Bulgarian church thus became closely associated with Byzantium. The services, like those in the other South Slav lands, were conducted in the language of the country; Church Slavonic was the earliest literary language of the Bulgarians.

The medieval period in Bulgarian history is dominated by quarrels with the Byzantine Empire. The Bulgarians also came into conflict with their other neighbor, the Serbs. At this time there commenced the Greek-Serbian-Bulgarian rivalry that has lasted to the present day. Then, as now, the prize at issue was Macedonia. Twice in the medieval period Bulgaria came close to achieving the conquest and incorporation of Constantinople, the capital of the Byzantine Empire.

The first attempt occurred during the reign of Simeon (893-927), when the Bulgarian Empire was a state of considerable territorial extent. Later it declined and Bulgaria fell under the rule of Constantinople. The second great period in medieval Bulgarian history began with the revolt of the Asen brothers, Peter and John, in 1186. Using the opportunity provided by the devastation inflicted upon Byzantium by the Crusaders, they laid the basis for the second Bulgarian Empire. In the reign of John Asen II (1218-41), Bulgaria controlled part of what is now Albania, northern Greece, and Serbia. As Bulgarian power again declined, parts of Bulgaria were conquered by Serbia.

THE SERBS. The first Serbian state was centered in the mountainous area of southern Serbia and Montenegro. Although Serbia was weaker than both the Bulgarian and Byzantine empires at first, a strong government and a Serbian dynasty were firmly established in the reign of Stevan Nemanja in the twelfth century. At the beginning of the thirteenth century, Stevan took the title of king; his brother, Sava, became the head of an independent Serbian Orthodox Church (an archbishopric linked with Byzantium). The greatest of the Serbian rulers, Stevan Dušan (1331-55), brought the medieval

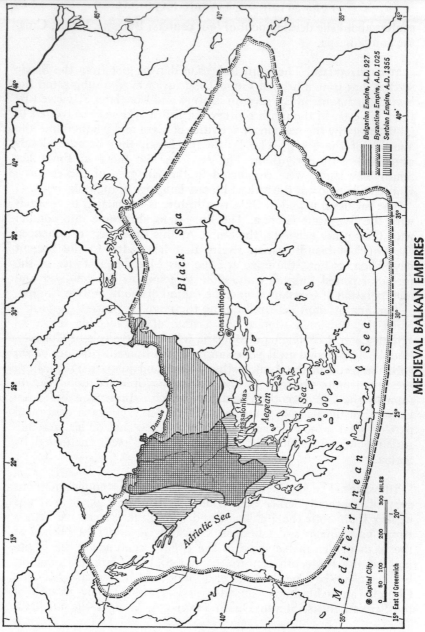

MEDIEVAL BALKAN EMPIRES

Bulgarian Empire, A.D. 927
Byzantine Empire, A.D. 1025
Serbian Empire, A.D. 1355

Black Sea

Constantinople

Danube

Thessaloniki

Aegean Sea

Adriatic Sea

Mediterranean Sea

● Capital City

East of Greenwich

0 50 100   200   300 MILES

20

state to the height of its power. After conquering the Bulgarians, he was able in 1346 to have himself crowned under the ambitious title of Emperor of the Serbs and Romans (i.e., Byzantium). He died while attempting to launch a campaign against Constantinople. Nevertheless, the conquest of the imperial city remained the ultimate ambition of both the Serbian and the Bulgarian rulers.

THE CROATS. Although both the Serbs and the Bulgars were drawn toward Constantinople, the source of their religious and political convictions and the goal of their imperial aspirations, the Croats became closely associated with Rome, Vienna, and Budapest. In the tenth century the Croats were able to establish an independent state which included Croatia and parts of Dalmatia. The country, however, soon fell under the power of Hungary. The Hungarians, or Magyars, were an Asiatic tribe related to the Huns and Avars. They settled in the Danubian region in the ninth century, established a strong political and military organization, and subsequently extended their control over neighboring areas. With the strong Venetian republic on one side and the Hungarians on the other, Croatia had little hope of maintaining an independent existence. In the twelfth century, military defeat and internal conflict led the Croatian nobility to accept Hungarian overlordship in return for a promise of political autonomy and the protection of the privileges of their class. The *Pacta Conventa* of 1102, one of the major documents in the history of the peoples of the Danubian region, contained the Croatian nobility's recognition of the king of Hungary as ruler of Croatia, with control of such matters as foreign affairs and defense. From the Croatian point of view, the union was nevertheless only personal; the king was to be represented by a viceroy, a *ban*, who was to live in Zagreb. In other administrative matters the Croats were to retain their autonomy. The interpretation to be given this agreement remained in dispute between the Croats and Hungarians throughout their common history. The federal form of union provided for in the *Pacta Conventa* remained that which the Croats preferred to maintain— whether with the Hungarians or, after 1918, with the Serbs. Too weak to form an independent state of their own, they wished to be part of a larger political unit, but with the right to administer their own internal affairs.

THE SLOVENES. The fourth South Slavic area, Slovenia, also enjoyed a period of national independence after 650. Thereafter it fell under

German rule. Like the Croats, the Slovenes were Catholic. Because Slovenia was closely associated with the more advanced Danubian civilization, conditions in the country remained superior to those in the rest of the Balkan world, particularly after most of the peninsula passed under Ottoman control. Until 1918, when the question of the formation of a Yugoslavia became acute, the Slovenes as a group played a rather passive role in the history of the Balkans.

THE BOSNIANS. The history of Bosnia is a turbulent and bloody one. Both Bosnia and her neighbor Hercegovina were briefly independent, but they soon became an object of bitter conflict between the Serbs and the Croats, between Orthodoxy and Catholicism. The sharp religious rivalry between the two major Christian organizations resulted in the rise of the Bogomilian heresy. The conflict also facilitated the Ottoman conquest of the fifteenth century and created a frame of mind within the provinces which resulted in later mass conversions to Islam.

THE ALBANIANS. Although the Albanians are of the most ancient racial stock of the Balkan peninsula, they failed to form a real political unity until modern times. A simple, pastoral people in a poor and mountainous country, they had little contact with the outside world. After the Ottoman conquest they appeared in the role of loyal soldiers of the sultan, and, later, as members of movements against Turkish rule. Their religious development had many points in common with that of the Bosnians. Conditions in the country were also propitious for mass conversions to Islam during the Ottoman occupation.

The Christian Balkan states on the eve of the Turkish conquest thus had many characteristics in common with the modern Balkan nations. The basic national patterns and the line of division between the Christian churches were established at that time and were not to be altered in the future. Serbia, Greece, Bulgaria, and the Danubian Principalities were drawn into the orbit of Constantinople and received their principal cultural and political imprint from the Byzantine Empire. Croatia, Slovenia, and Dalmatia came under German, Italian, and Hungarian influence. The major rivalries of Balkan history also made their appearance in the medieval period. The Greek-Bulgarian-Serbian quarrel over Macedonia is perhaps the most important of these, but the Croatian conflicts with Hungary and Italy and the Rumanian-Hungarian struggle over Transylvania also originated at this time.

When the Balkan nations began their fight for national liberation in the nineteenth and twentienth centuries, the medieval period assumed a new significance. Deprived of an independent modern history, the nations naturally turned back to the time when they had been both strong and free. The medieval heritage gave the Balkan peoples a feeling of identity and pride, but it also provided the basis for continued conflict. The rivalries of the past and the old claims on disputed territories were revived and carried over into the new age. The Bulgarian Empire of Simeon, the Serbian Empire of Dušan, and the Byzantine Empire under Basil II all covered roughly the same territory. In the modern period each of these rulers often remained the hero of his nation and the limits of his empire were accepted as the correct boundaries for the state.

THREE

THE OTTOMAN CONQUEST:
THE SUBJUGATION OF BALKAN NATIONALITY

The Establishment of Ottoman Rule

In the second half of the fourteenth century the warring Christian states paid the price of disunity and lost their freedom to a Moslem nation that took full advantage of the situation. At the end of the thirteenth century, a settlement of Turks was established near the Sea of Marmora; around 1300 one of their chiefs, Osman or Othman, took the title of Sultan. From his name is derived that of the Ottoman Empire. In the middle of the next century, a great era of conquest was commenced. It should be noted that the Ottoman armies first won victories in Europe before turning to the subjugation of Asia Minor. Their attack on Constantinople was delayed until the Balkan hinterland was secured. The fall of Adrianople in 1361 was followed by the acquisition of parts of Bulgaria. On June 28, 1389, in the most significant of the battles of that time, an army of Serbs, Bulgarians, Albanians, and Bosnians met defeat at Kosovo, an event which brought an end to Serbian independence. This date, Vidovdan or St. Vitus' Day, became thereafter the Serbian national holiday. This anniversary was preserved through song and story and was to retain a particular significance in Serbian history. After the conquest of Serbia, Bulgaria succumbed. Then the Turkish armies marched on to the Rumanian lands and, during the next century, Wallachia was reduced to the status of a vassal state.

In the organization of its conquests, the Ottoman government

24

allowed Serbia some autonomy at first, but Bulgaria became at once a Turkish province under direct Ottoman rule. In the future the Bulgarians, largely because of their geographic position, continued to bear the heaviest of the burdens of foreign occupation. Their national awakening, consequently, was to be delayed until after that of their neighbors.

At the beginning of the fifteenth century, the surge of Ottoman conquest was briefly halted by the armies of Tamerlane. At the time the Turks also had to face the problem of the control of the Mediterranean. Like nineteenth-century Britain, the Italian city-state of Venice had in the fifteenth century developed a great commercial sea empire in the Mediterranean. Until the destruction of its power in the Napoleonic Wars, Venice played a major role in the history of the Balkans and the Near East. At various times, she was able to control Dalmatia, the Morea, Crete, Cyprus, and other islands. The Ottoman Empire, primarily a land power, was forced to construct a fleet to meet the Venetian challenge.

The greatest single Ottoman military achievement took place during the reign of Mohammed II (1451-81). In 1453 Constantinople was captured, bringing an end to the Byzantine Empire. Although Byzantium had by then been reduced to little more than the capital city and its surrounding territory, the conquest had immense symbolic significance. Even under Ottoman rule, Constantinople maintained a particular meaning for Christians. The fall of the city marked the definite accomplishment of the subjugation of the Balkans. The Ottoman Empire now controlled Serbia, Bosnia, Bulgaria, and most of Greece. Resistance was offered in Albania by the brave leader, Skanderbeg, but this region also finally succumbed. The single area in the Balkans which maintained its independence for most of the period was the state of Montenegro, a mountainous region which became a refuge for those who refused to accept Moslem rule. Although Montenegro was of little economic, political, or military value to the Christian world, its constant struggle for freedom and its harassment of the Turks won it the admiration of the subjugated Balkan peoples.

The reign of Suleiman the Magnificent (1520-66) marked the summit of Moslem power and prestige. Under his leadership, Ottoman armies again moved northward, this time against the king of Hungary. In 1521 Belgrade fell; in 1526, at the battle of Mohacs, the Hungarian Kosovo, the Magyar forces were also conquered and that country remained under Ottoman rule for almost 150 years. In 1529 the armies of Suleiman reached the gates of Vienna, but at that point their advance in Europe was halted. For more than a century and a half, Vienna stood as the protector of Christian Europe against the Moslem forces.

Because this survey deals with the Balkans, no attempt will be made to discuss Ottoman victories in Asia and Africa. The accompanying map shows the extent and grandeur of Suleiman's domain. The splendor of his military triumphs was matched by a high level of domestic achievement. After his reign, however, the Ottoman Empire lost the swift impulsion and drive which had hitherto characterized its development. Although it surrendered no territory to Christian Europe until 1683, the vigor and zeal which had characterized its previous history slowly declined.

Ottoman Administration in the Balkans

Ottoman rule, the common historical experience of all the Balkan peoples, suffers from a singularly bad reputation. This condition arises partially from the tradition of nationalistic historical writing which developed in all the Balkan states soon after their liberation, when the sufferings and hardships of the past were still clearly remembered. In addition, the empire is usually judged on the basis of a study of conditions during the final two centuries of its existence. In the reign of Suleiman, the Ottoman Empire was equal to any other great state of the time. Suleiman was a worthy contemporary of Charles V, Henry VIII, and Francis I. Moreover, in certain respects —notably religious toleration—the empire was much superior to the Catholic and Protestant states of Europe. The government was, however, organized on principles different from those of the West and its structure was entirely foreign to European political concepts.

It is first to be strongly emphasized that this was a Moslem, not a Turkish, empire; its rulers thought of themselves as belonging to a religious group, not a national one. Any Christian member of the Ottoman Empire was free to join the privileged class simply by changing his faith, although the Turks did not attempt to force conversions. In fact, in only three of the conquered regions were there notable conversions to Islam. In Bosnia and Albania, both areas of religious strife between the Christian churches, it has been estimated that 70 per cent of the people became Moslems. In Crete, perhaps half the population was converted. There were also many

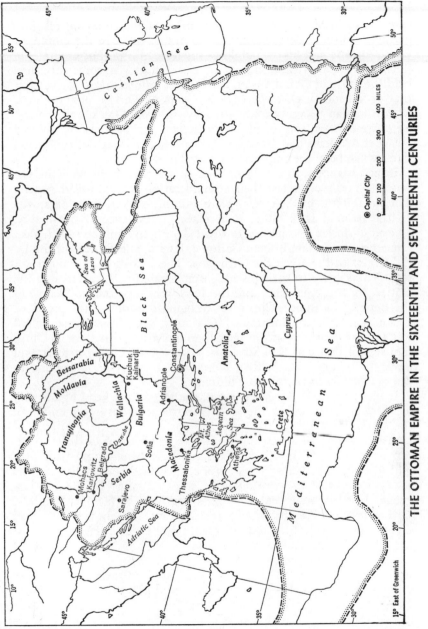

THE OTTOMAN EMPIRE IN THE SIXTEENTH AND SEVENTEENTH CENTURIES

27

conversions in Macedonia. Once a member of the dominant religious group, the former Christian could attain any office in the empire to which fortune and his own abilities might lead him. For example, in the 170 years after the conquest of Constantinople, some fifty men held the office of Grand Vizier, the highest administrative office after that of the sultan. Of these, only five were of Turkish origin: eleven were Albanian; eleven were South Slav; six were Greek; and the rest were Armenian, Georgian, and even Italian. It should also be pointed out that Moslems and Christians alike suffered from the evil conditions which beset the empire in its period of decline.

In accordance with their emphasis on religious principles, the Ottoman officials organized their administration on the *millet* system. The inhabitants of the empire were administered by units organized on the basis of faith rather than place of residence or nationality. The non-Moslem peoples were divided into five millets: Orthodox, Gregorian Armenian, Roman Catholic, Jewish, and Protestant. By far the largest of these was the Orthodox. The Christians, although not regarded as equal to the Moslems, were treated with remarkable toleration for the time. They and the Jews were regarded as "People of the Book" (the Bible); Christ was recognized as one of the prophets, although inferior to Mohammed. Certainly, the Moslem government was far more tolerant of the Jews than any European state or Christian sect of that era. Non-Moslems, however, were subject to certain grave disabilities, notably their liability to a special head tax and to the *devshirme*, or the tax in children.

Under this system of government, the recognized head of any millet was, understandably, the leader of the religious community. In the Orthodox Church, this position was held by the Patriarch of Constantinople, who was now considered also an official of the Ottoman Empire. Although the Patriarch held titular supremacy over all Orthodox Christians in the empire, each Orthodox nation had its own ecclesiastical organization and conducted services in its own language. The Bulgarian center was at Ohrid; the Serbian, at Peć. The Orthodox churches throughout the Balkans thus became national organizations, reflecting and representing the particular interests of the individual Balkan people. The universality and independence of secular authority aimed at by the Roman Catholic Church thus had no counterpart in the Orthodox Church under Ottoman rule. Here religion and nationality went hand in hand. The Orthodox nations sought and needed separate religious organizations. Although the Ottoman officials regarded the Christians as one religious group, the administration of the Orthodox Church was in fact divided along national lines.

The millet system thus preserved for the Christians a measure of self-government and national individuality. The Ottoman rulers were chiefly concerned with raising money from their Christian subjects to govern, defend, or expand the empire. They did not regard many aspects of local government as within their province. Such matters as education, health, and even the administration of justice usually fell to local authorities. A strong tradition of self-government was therefore built up in various parts of the empire, particularly in the Morea and in parts of Serbia and Bulgaria.

At first, the effects of the Ottoman conquest upon the Balkan peasant was not entirely negative, when one considers the violent and cruel nature of the age. The Ottoman cavalry, the strongest element in the Ottoman military forces of the time, was supported by a system of land-holding. In return for a nonhereditary grant of land, the *timar*, the cavalryman was bound to serve the sultan on call. He was allowed to collect only certain specified taxes from the peasants on his estates. As long as the system was maintained as originally conceived, the peasant on the Turkish estates carried fewer burdens and obligations than the serf in western Europe. With the degeneration of the empire, the conditions of the timar system also changed and the position of the peasant declined.

Of particular interest was the participation of the converted Christian in the organization and defense of the entire empire. By the time of Suleiman, the administration of the state had been put in the hands of slave officials, who were acquired by outright purchase, chosen from among the prisoners of war, or selected from the Christian children taken from their parents through the devshirme system. Approximately every five years, one out of every four boys between the ages of ten and twenty among the Christian population could be taken as a form of tribute. The children were then converted to Islam, and the most promising were sent to the Palace School in Constantinople. The ablest among them eventually rose to fill the highest positions in the empire. They became generals, provincial governors, and even Grand Viziers. The system can be regarded either as a terrible misfortune inflicted upon the Christian families or as a magnificent opportunity for an able child to escape the raw and brutal life of his village. At home his opportunities were pitifully limited; in Constantinople he could rise to administer the empire.

The devshirme system was also used to fill the ranks of the most famous of the Ottoman military organizations, the Janissaries. This dedicated, fanatic military corps, composed primarily of the converted children of Christians, became a privileged elite. Its members were not allowed to marry and, until the corps underwent a process of decomposition and degeneration, it was the principal military support of the empire.

Although former Christians thus dominated the military and administrative organs of the state, Moslem society, through a parallel set of institutions, controlled matters pertaining to the Moslem faith, law, and education. Through these institutions and through the sultan and his entourage, the Moslem community held firm control over the empire. This remarkable system of government, in which the administration was carried on by a slave cadre, could succeed only as long as the master class remained strong and able.

Most important was the person of the sultan. In the years before Suleiman, the empire had enjoyed a line of remarkably able rulers. After Suleiman's reign, the government began to weaken from the center—"fish rot from the head," as the Turkish proverb explained it. Particularly unfortunate was a change in the law of succession which made the oldest member of the imperial family, rather than the first son of the sultan, the heir to the throne. The result of this change was a succession of weak rulers who were controlled by strong advisers.

The Decline of the Empire

As the center of government lost strength, the provinces gradually assumed more importance. By the late eighteenth and early nineteenth centuries, certain local administrators, such as Ali Pasha of Janina and Mohammed Ali of Egypt, were able to exercise virtually independent power. The decline of the central government was accompanied by a gradual increase in corruption throughout the entire administration. Ability, which had once characterized the slave personnel recruited under the devshirme system, no longer determined advancement; offices were awarded to favorites or sold outright. An official who received a post under these circumstances naturally regarded his appointment as an opportunity for personal enrichment. He fleeced those below him and sold the offices under his control. The tax system, in particular, suffered in these circumstances. The task of collecting taxes was generally farmed out, and most of the money collected disappeared before it reached the central treasury. As Ottoman administration deteriorated, the Christian peasants and townspeople began to suffer the miserable consequences of bad government. The taxes became extortionate. The provincial governors were more interested in enriching themselves than in correctly administering their territories. The police too often robbed rather than protected the people. The official institutions of the state no longer could be relied upon to protect the individual from injustice and violence.

Not only did the internal administration of the state decline but, even more important for the integrity of the empire, the military forces also deteriorated. The Janissary corps, the finest section of the Ottoman armies, changed in character and composition. As might have been expected, the members of the corps eventually sought the right to marry, to found families, and to enroll their sons in the privileged organization. The army thus lost its unique character. No longer a force of fanatic converts, willing to risk their lives for their faith, the Janissary corps became a body of men chiefly interested in their own advancement, comfort, and prosperity. Equally serious was the failure of the Janissaries—in fact, of all the Ottoman forces—to keep pace with the advances made in the West in military technology and in strategy. The intensely conservative nature of the corps was revealed in its aversion to military or political change. Because of its military power and prestige, the corps was also a political force. It was able to interfere in the government and it had the power to overthrow a sultan. Thus, instead of forming a shield for the empire, the corps became another element contributing to its decline.

The individual peasant was also affected by changes in the conditions of land-holding. The timar system was gradually replaced by the *chiflik* system. The Moslem warrior, who had formerly held his land in return for military service, now acquired hereditary control of his property. The peasant was simultaneously reduced to the status of a serf, and he could expect no protection from the local Ottoman administration against the whims or arbitrary levies of his overlord. Peasant discontent and open revolt naturally increased. At times of extreme disorder, the Christian peasant could always retreat to the mountains, where, although life was hard, the individual was free. Only with great difficulty could he be reached there by the soldier, the police, or the tax collector. These conditions resulted in the depopulation of large areas. Contemporary travelers were often greatly impressed by the lack of habitation in areas of clear agricultural value.

The same conditions contributed to bring about another development: the denationalization of the larger towns. Throughout the Balkans, the Moslem administrators and landowners controlled the most valuable property. They formed an important proportion of the population of the relatively few major towns. The development of commercial life throughout the empire in the eighteenth century added another element to the life of the towns. Trade came to be handled not by Turks, Rumanians, or South Slavs, but by Greeks, Jews, and Armenians. The principal trading towns thus often took on a national character different from that of the surrounding countryside. For example, large Greek populations could be found in towns along the coast of the Black Sea, in Bulgaria, and in Macedonia; Thessaloniki had a Jewish majority in the nineteenth century.

The flight of the peasants into the mountains brought about a condition which became most important in Balkan history and to the Balkan outlook. With the failure of the state to secure law and order within its boundaries, brigandage became a widespread phenomenon. No merchant or traveler ventured on the Balkan highways without the company of armed guards. The people themselves were forced to live closely together. As a nineteenth-century traveler reported: "Nowhere . . . are isolated houses to be found; for the good reason that, if there were, the owners would have their throats cut in a week." [1] Under these circumstances, the inhabitants were forced to take countermeasures for the protection of their lives and property. Throughout Balkan history, the *hajduk* (as he is known in the Slavic lands) or the *klepht* (as he is called in Greece) has been a figure of great attraction and the hero of popular songs and legends. The *hajduk*, a Balkan Robin Hood, kept alive the hope of the Christians, and later formed an important element in the wars of liberation. The idea of the lone fighter against tyranny and the glorification of guerrilla

[1] Henry C. Barkley, *Between the Danube and the Black Sea, or, Five Years in Bulgaria* (London: John Murray, Publishers, Ltd., 1876), p. 19.

warfare, which appear again in modern times, have a long tradition in
Balkan history.

It should also be emphasized that the vices of corruption, maladministration, violence, and injustice figured not only in the relation-
ships between the rulers and their subjects, but also entered into the
dealings of the subjects with one another. The Ottoman Empire thus
gave to all its members lessons in government which had been better
avoided. Many of the worst elements of Turkish rule were, in fact,
carried over into the administration of the new Balkan states simply
because the people themselves had had no other political experience. When generations have lived under rapacious governors, the
idea that corruption is an inevitable attribute of public office is not
easily eradicated.

Perhaps the worst feature of the long centuries of Ottoman rule
was not the bad government to which the Balkan people were subjected, but the fact that Ottoman rule cut them off from western
Europe at a time when that region was experiencing a tremendous
upsurge. Until Suleiman's death in 1566, it can be argued that the
internal development of the Ottoman Empire had kept pace with
that of Europe. Thereafter, however, Ottoman progress, in the Western sense of the term, nearly ceased. For almost three centuries the
inhabitants of the Balkan peninsula lived in intellectual isolation and
under extremely primitive conditions, cut off from the mainstream of
European life. The changes in European living standards and outlook
brought about by the scientific, intellectual, and industrial revolutions affected only an extremely limited group in the Balkan peninsula. The majority of the people were never brought into direct contact with the framework of concepts upon which Western development rested.

While isolating the Balkans from Europe, Ottoman civilization
offered little to the Christian in return. The Ottoman Turk was a
warrior, not a builder. The visitor to the Balkans today is repeatedly
struck by the lack of physical evidence of the almost five-hundred-
year-long-occupation. A nineteenth-century British observer wrote:

> Where are the monuments of power and the energy of the mighty
> people who laid the Christian Empire of the East in the dust? Where
> are the proofs that they have for four centuries held dominion over
> one of the most beautiful and fertile countries in our hemisphere?

Where?—The undrained marsh, the sand-choked river, the grass-grown marketplace, the deserted field, the crumbling fortress, the broken arch; these re-echo: Where! [2]

The Great Powers and the Eastern Question

How, under these conditions, was the Ottoman Empire able to hold on to so much of its territory for so long? Just as the divisions among the Christian Balkan states had facilitated the Ottoman conquest, so the conflicts among the states of Europe allowed the continuance of Moslem control over the Balkans even when the empire itself was militarily and politically weak. In every period before World War I, the empire was able to find allies and protectors among the European powers who wished to use it as a counterweight against a strong opponent. The problem of the decline of Turkey and the diplomatic complications which ensued are generally referred to as "the Eastern Question." The entire problem played a predominant role in European diplomacy, particularly in the nineteenth century.

Francis I of France opened relations between Turkey and the West when he sought the cooperation of the sultan against the Habsburg Empire. The Capitulations of 1535 opened the Ottoman Empire to French trade. Holland and Britain made similar agreements soon afterward. The Ottoman Empire thus became part of the European balance-of-power system. At this time, France attempted to unite Sweden, Poland, and Turkey into a diplomatic front that would outflank the Habsburg Empire. In the eighteenth century, this combination could also be used against Russia.

Although the great wave of Ottoman conquest ended with the reign of Suleiman, small acquisitions were made later. Cyprus and Crete were taken from Venice and some territory from Poland. For over a century the empire was able to hold its lands together and in 1683 it mounted a final great offensive against central Europe. The seige of Vienna in that year marked the turning point; thereafter it was Europe that made gains against the empire. The diplomatic situation was strongly altered at the end of the seventeenth century, when Russia joined Venice and Austria in the attempt to throw back Ottoman power. In 1689 a grand alliance of Austria, Venice, Poland,

---

[2] Edmund Spencer, *Travels in European Turkey in 1850, through Bosnia, Servia, Bulgaria, Macedonia, Thrace, Albania, and Epirus, etc.* (London: Colburn and Co., 1851), I, 2.

and Russia was formed. In the following year the Porte[3] was forced to make its first major territorial concessions. In the next two hundred years, five principal agreements were signed by the Ottoman Empire: Karlowitz (Karlovac, 1699), Kuchuk Kainardji (1774), Bucharest (1812), Adrianople (1829), and Berlin (1878). Each of these treaties pushed the Turkish boundaries further south. The first, the Treaty of Karlowitz, gave Austria most of Hungary, Transylvania, Croatia, and Slavonia. Venice received Dalmatia and the Morea, which she held until 1718. Poland also gained territory. Further campaigns were waged against the Turks in 1716-18 and 1736-39, but similar successes were not achieved. It was not until the reign of Catherine the Great of Russia that another series of great offensives was directed against Constantinople.

In the previous period the Habsburg Empire had led the western forces; now Russia became the chief opponent of Turkey and consequently the strongest supporter of the Christian people in their fight for independence. An active policy against Turkey was inaugurated by Peter the Great at the beginning of the eighteenth century, with his plans for expansion toward the Black Sea and the encouragement he gave to Balkan revolt. His policy was carried on by his successors and, as a result, the Balkan peoples came to look to Russia as their strongest protector among the European powers. The initial great Russian successes were won in the reign of Catherine the Great. In 1768 she began the first of her wars against the Ottoman Empire. It was concluded by the Treaty of Kuchuk Kainardji (1774), the most important for modern Balkan history of the agreements negotiated between Russia and Turkey. In this treaty Russia gained some territory along the Black Sea, but, more significant, she was able thereafter to claim, because of the ambiguous wording of the pact, the right to speak in behalf of the Orthodox Christians of the Ottoman Empire. Although the real intent of the stipulations was clear to no one, including the Russian government, Russia at times used them to claim a protectorship over the Orthodox Balkan peoples. A second war, waged in 1787 in cooperation with Joseph II of Austria, was not so successful, but by the time of her death (1796) Catherine had

[3] The Ottoman Empire was regularly referred to in diplomatic correspondence as *the Porte*. The Sublime Porte was the designation for the gateway leading to the building which contained the principal offices of the government in Constantinople.

won large stretches of territory, made Russia the dominant power in the Black Sea, and laid the foundation for future Russian championship of Balkan Orthodoxy.

The plans of both Russia and Austria for eastern expansion were interrupted by the French Revolution and the Napoleonic Wars. For the next few years, the attention of Europe was turned toward combatting French power and the political influences of the French Revolution. Two aspects of the complicated diplomatic maneuvering of the period are of significance for Balkan history. First, in 1804 and 1809 France took from Austria and Venice the lands of Istria, Slovenia, Dalmatia, and parts of Croatia—all of which were inhabited by South Slavs—and formed from these the so-called Illyrian Provinces. The reforms associated with the French Revolution were incorporated into the government. This state, the first modern political union of the South Slavs, lasted only a short time, but it inspired later movements for unity in the area. The second event of significance was the conclusion of the Treaty of Bucharest (1812). Under the terms of this agreement, the Moldavian province of Bessarabia was incorporated into the Russian Empire. Since then, Rumania's rival claim to this territory has played a major role in the relations between the two states.

In the treaties of Vienna of 1815, which ended the long years of warfare in Europe, Austria received the former Venetian possessions in Dalmatia, which further increased the number of South Slav peoples within her boundaries. Between 1699 and 1815 she had already acquired lands inhabited by Croats and Slovenes. She also had a large population of Serbs, particularly in the area of the Vojvodina. These people had fled into the region north of the Sava River to escape Turkish domination and had been permanently settled there by Vienna in an attempt to establish a military frontier defended by local inhabitants. This region thereafter became a vigorous center of Serbian national life. The capital was Novi Sad, a city not far from Belgrade, which was still under Ottoman rule. Close by, in Karlowitz, lived the Patriarch of the Serbian Orthodox Church.

The Congress of Vienna marked the end of an era of diplomacy. All the major states were weary of war and of the social and political experimentation which had been brought about by the spread of the concepts of the French Revolution. The European governments wished for a period of tranquillity in which to recover from the quarter-century of war they had experienced. Although the great powers wanted an end to international discord, the subjugated nationalities of the Balkans were not in a similar mood. The French Revolution had brought a new spirit to Europe and the ideology of the time gave a theoretical justification to Balkan rebellion. The age was indeed, in an intellectual and emotional sense, fitted for the rise of Balkan nationalism. The Romantic Movement of the post-Vienna era gave further impetus to the liberation movement through its emphasis on the past and on the nation. The revolutionary ferment in the Balkans, however, soon ran into conflict with the politics of the great powers, which feared its political and international implications. Through most of the period, the chief concern of the powers was not the welfare or fate of the Balkan Christians or the Ottoman Turks, but the fear that a breakup of the Ottoman Empire would result in too great an extension of Russian power.

In the eighteenth century Britain won the duel for empire with France; in 1815 she saw her rival's military power destroyed. She was thereafter the greatest of the colonial nations and the European balance of power had been established once more. Although many British statesmen were skeptical about the real benefit to be derived from colonial possessions, the protection of these territories—and even their extension—became a major consideration in British foreign policy. In addition, British trade and commerce in the east continued to be of prime importance. A principal British trade route ran through the eastern Mediterranean; trade relations with Constantinople were also good. The protection of India, Britain's prize colonial possession, was also intimately bound with the question of British naval supremacy in the eastern Mediterranean. Although the weak condition of the Ottoman Empire was recognized, the British government could see no alternative to its continued existence. It was feared that, should the empire fall, Russia would inevitably fill the vacuum thereby created in the Balkans. Most British statesmen did not believe that independent Balkan states would be able to withstand the sustained pressure of their great neighbor. They recognized the strong religious bonds which connected Russia with the Rumanians, the Bulgarians, the Serbs, and the Greeks and the appeal of Slavic brotherhood which attracted the South Slavs to the northern power. The British government, therefore, sought to maintain the empire, but also to dominate it and to sponsor the introduction of measures which would better the position of Christians within it. Three times in the nineteenth century—in 1839, in 1856, and in 1876—under strong foreign, especially British, pressure, the Ottoman government issued reform decrees designed to improve the administration of the country and the lot of the subject nationalities. None of these acts was ever put into effective practice. All were subverted from the top. However, even when it was clear that genuine reform was not possible, Britain preferred usually the continued maladministration on the Balkan peninsula to the danger of a possible upset of the balance of power in the East.

Russia was in a more difficult position, for her interests in the area conflicted. After 1815, during the reigns of tsars Alexander I (1801-25) and Nicholas I (1825-55), Russia became the defender of the autocratic governments on the continent of Europe threatened by revolutionary activities and one of the chief supporters of the Vienna settlement of 1815. This policy was in accord with her interests in central Europe. She could not, therefore, give outright approval to national revolutions in the Balkans and at the same time support the suppression of similar movements in Poland, Italy, and Germany. It was, nevertheless, difficult for her to ignore or to condemn these activities. In the eighteenth century, commencing with the reign of Peter the Great, the Russian government had, in fact, declared itself the sponsor and protector of Balkan Orthodox Christianity; the Balkan peoples expected Russian assistance. There was also much popular sympathy within Russia for the Balkan Christians. Moreover, although the annexation of the Balkan lands of the Ottoman Empire was not a goal of Russian policy, practical advantages were to be derived from the general diplomatic situation. Undoubtedly, the liberated people would be sincere and grateful friends of their powerful patron. The military position of Russia would thereby be strengthened and she would gain allies against both Britain and the Habsburg Empire. Throughout the nineteenth century, Russian policy remained divided on the question of supporting Balkan liberation movements and on the degree of control which should or should not be exercised in a state once it had been freed from Ottoman rule.

The Russo-British antagonism centered on the problem of the control of the Turkish Straits. Unlike Russia, Britain did not have an army within striking distance of Constantinople. She could exert pressure there only through her Mediterranean fleet. This force was challenged chiefly by the Russian Black Sea fleet, which could enter the Mediterranean only through the narrow channel controlled by the Ottoman Empire. Throughout the nineteenth century, Britain sought to obtain an international agreement which would close the Straits to Russian warships. For a short time after the Crimean War, she was even able to enforce the demilitarization of the entire Black Sea. This one-sided arrangement provided a counterweight for the Russian land army and reinforced the British route to India. The Russian government naturally disputed such unilateral arrangements, but it did not, in principle, object to the closing of the Straits to all warships, including her own. Because Russian naval power was always inferior to the British, and because the Black Sea coastal areas were open to invasion, Russia felt that she could benefit from regulations which prevented British and French warships from entering the Black Sea, even if she were thereby herself excluded from the eastern Mediterranean.

These complications between the great powers had enormous significance for the Balkan peoples. Because of the conditions of the time, they needed outside assistance—or, at least, outside indifference—for the success of their national movements. The European governments were deeply concerned about the Balkan question, but they naturally based their policy on their own individual interests, which usually meant that they supported the status quo. Thus the Ottoman Empire, the state with the worst administrative system in Europe, dragged on for another century after 1815. Nevertheless, specific international situations did arise in this period which allowed the gradual freeing of the Balkan nations.

The Balkan People under Ottoman Rule

The account of the national liberation movements must be preceded by an analysis of the development of each nationality under Ottoman rule. As has been noted, not all Christians were injured by the system, nor did all Moslems benefit. The Anatolian Turkish peasant suffered as much as his Balkan Christian counterpart from bad government and extortion. Among the Christian population itself, the fate of the different national groups varied widely.

THE GREEKS. Certainly, of the Christian peoples, the Greeks fared best. In the eighteenth and nineteenth centuries they achieved what has been described as "a senior partnership" [4] in the Ottoman Empire. It was not, however, the ordinary Greek peasant who enjoyed

---

[4] A. J. Toynbee, A *Study of History* (London: Oxford University Press, H. Milford, 1935), II, 225.

this position; he, like others of his class in all parts of the Balkans, lived in misery and usually worked for a Turkish or Greek landowner. Rather, it was the Greek who settled in Constantinople, or who became a merchant with interests throughout the Mediterranean, who now came to form a privileged stratum within the empire. Greeks also penetrated the administrative system of the state, particularly in the eighteenth century. The best-educated of the Christians, they were notably adept at foreign languages, which the Turks considered beneath their dignity to learn. Because of their capabilities, Greeks came to hold three important posts: Grand Dragoman (chief interpreter), Dragoman of the Fleet, and the hospodarships (governorships) of Moldavia and Wallachia. These Greeks, known as Phanariotes, after the quarter in which they lived in Constantinople, were not only powerful but also exceedingly corrupt.

Greek nationals also dominated the higher offices of the Orthodox Church. Because, under the millet system, officials of the Orthodox Church were also administrators in the Ottoman state, Greek influence here was particularly significant. Greek became increasingly the language of the Orthodox Church and also of education, which was closely associated with it. There thus developed a type of Greek ecclesiastical imperialism which operated to the detriment of the native elements in the Slavic and Rumanian lands. The national liberation movements in Bulgaria and in the Rumanian principalities, in particular, were directed against both Turkish and Greek influence. The Christian world, therefore, was not united. The Greeks, under the cover of Ottoman power, were able to extend their influence over other Christians.

The Orthodox Church in the Ottoman Empire in time became, like the other branches of the government, thoroughly corrupt. The office of Patriarch and all the lower positions were for sale to the highest bidder. Between 1623 and 1700, the Patriarchate of Constantinople changed hands approximately fifty times. Thus the church, as such, did not offer to its members an example of moral rectitude or of good administration, but it would have been almost impossible for any ecclesiastic organization not to have fallen victim to the general conditions in the empire.

The Greeks held one more great advantage in their relations with other Balkan peoples: their commercial supremacy. Particular gains were made at the end of the eighteenth century when they were allowed to sail under the Russian flag while their French and British rivals fought each other in the wars of the time. It was this merchant group that came into closest contact with the ideas of the West and furnished the leadership for the national liberation movement.

THE RUMANIANS. After the Greeks, it was perhaps the Rumanians who held the best position under Ottoman rule. Unlike the lands of the South Slavs, the principalities of Moldavia and Wallachia were, at least in theory, never incorporated into the empire; instead, they remained tributary provinces. Turkish troops occupied certain points and large tributes in money and produce were regularly collected. The political and economic development of these provinces took a course different from that of the rest of the Balkans and more closely resembled that of Hungary and Poland. The Principalities had a native aristocracy and the land was organized into large estates which were worked by an enserfed peasantry.

At first, both Moldavia and Wallachia had the right to choose their own rulers, but this privilege was lost when Moldavia supported Peter the Great in one of his campaigns against the Porte. Thereafter the governorships of the provinces were given to Phanariote Greeks, who used them as a means of personal enrichment. Because the posts were so lucrative, they changed hands frequently. Thus, for example, between 1714 and 1821 there were thirty-six governors in Moldavia and forty-one in Wallachia. The corruption at the top spread throughout the entire administrative system. This alien rule, corrupt and inefficient, was naturally deeply resented by the Rumanians, although they were accustomed to no higher political morality. The friction between Greek and Rumania later affected the history of both peoples.

The Rumanian population in Transylvania, together with the Hungarians, fell under direct Ottoman rule in the sixteenth century. This domination ceased after the Treaty of Karlowitz, when the province, like Hungary, became part of the Habsburg Empire. In the next few years Transylvania became closely tied with Hungary. A similar political fate befell the majority of the Croats, who, after the defeat of the Turks, became a part of the Austrian Empire and maintained particularly close associations with Budapest.

THE SERBS. The position of the Serbs, unlike that of the Greeks and the Rumanians, was distinctly unfavorable. Their land was long a battlefield for the Turkish and Austrian armies. At the time of the conquest the Ottoman victors had eliminated the old Serbian ruling class; the Serbs thus remained a peasant people with little possibility of contact with the outside world. Unlike the Rumanians and the Greeks, as individuals they were not in a position to acquire wealth or education. Even the Serbian Orthodox Church, which had effectively served to preserve the national identity, was weakened in the eighteenth century when the Patriarchate was abolished. At the end of the seventeenth century, the Serbian Patriarch and 30,000 of his followers, who had supported Austria in the wars, were forced to flee with the retreating Austrian troops across the Sava River. They subsequently settled near Karlowitz. In retaliation for the Serbian defection, the sultan thereafter appointed Greeks as the Patriarchs of Peć. The latter, in 1766, recommended the abolition of the Serbian Patriarchate, whose authority and functions then came under the jurisdiction of the Greek ecumenical Patriarchate at Constantinople. Because of this and other developments, the first center of the Serbian national movement was to be within the Habsburg Empire at Novi Sad and Karlowitz, and not in Serbia proper.

THE BULGARIANS. Of all of the Balkan peoples under Ottoman domination, the Bulgarians were in the least favorable position. Not only were their lands close to Constantinople, but the control of their territory was a military necessity for the Ottoman state. The tax burden they bore was all the heavier and they suffered longer from the general corruption and maladministration of the Ottoman rule. Unlike the Greeks and the Serbs, they could not so easily escape into isolated regions in times of disaster. Moreover, in the eighteenth century, they, like the Serbs, found the position of their national church lowered. The Bulgarian ecclesiastical jurisdiction at Ohrid was abolished in 1767, a year after the abolition of the Serbian Patriarchate at Peć. Greek control was then established both over church affairs and over education. Greek merchants also had a strong position in the commercial life of the country. There were no Bulgarian schools and no Bulgarian books or journals. The Bulgarian nationalist, in his struggle for independence, thus fought against Greek control as well as against Ottoman rule.

This brief sketch of Balkan life under the Turks illustrates the conditions underlying the developments of the nineteenth century. Under Ottoman rule, the Balkan peoples continued their separate lives. Neither the fact that they were under a single power, nor the tendency of the ruling Moslems to regard them as a single Christian group brought them together. The educated and privileged people, the Greeks, used their position—not to secure Christian unity—but to try to strengthen and extend the jurisdiction of organizations they controlled and to establish the Greek language in education and government. The unfortunate results of these policies became clear in the age of national liberation. Not only did the Balkan peoples generally fail to aid each other, but, after attaining national freedom, all entered into bitter disputes with their neighbors. Their common suffering under foreign domination thus did not provide a firm basis for later cooperation.

FOUR

THE NATIONAL LIBERATION MOVEMENTS:

THE FORMATION OF THE MODERN

BALKAN STATES

National Revival

In the years between 1806 and 1878, despite a difficult international situation, the Serbians, the Greeks, the Rumanians, and the
Bulgarians were able to establish independent or autonomous states.
In each case, however, significant numbers of the national population
were left outside the boundaries of the new nations. As a result, the
initial struggle for an independent government was followed in each
country by continued agitation for further expansion. The drawing of
boundaries was singularly difficult in the Balkans. In the days of
Ottoman rule the different nationalities had moved freely within the
empire. Moreover, certain groups had tended to specialize in certain
functions. The commercial predominance of the Greeks, the Jews,
and the Armenians gave some of the towns of Bulgaria and Macedonia a Greek character despite the overwhelmingly Slavic countryside.
The Kutzo-Vlachs, related to the Rumanians, followed the occupation of shepherd in Greece and elsewhere. A Turkish population was
also to be found, particularly in Macedonia, Greece, and Bulgaria.

It was often very difficult to determine nationality. The great majority of the Balkan peoples lived as poverty-stricken peasants in
small, isolated villages. They were, in general, illiterate, spoke local
dialects, and they had no means of following the political events of
the world. Although a large degree of local government was to be
found on the village level, it was patriarchal in character. The peasant was a member first of a family, second of a specific village, and

third of either the Orthodox or Catholic faith. The question of nationality, the fourth consideration, was clear when the individual lived in a compact national unit, but it was often difficult to determine in border areas. In the Balkans, as elsewhere, the principal criteria for nationality were, first, language, and, second, religion. This standard divided the Rumanian from the South Slav, and the South Slav from the Greek. It was more difficult to establish a clear line between Serb and Bulgar because both peoples were Orthodox and the two languages are similar. In the nineteenth century, other criteria were introduced, particularly by the Greeks, who claimed territories inhabited by Slavic-speaking peoples. It was argued that historical and cultural factors should also be considered—that it was possible to speak another language, but to feel oneself part of the Greek nation. In general, however, it was language—together with a feeling of identity with the group—that provided the logical basis for the establishment of lines of division between the different peoples.

Although the Balkan nations followed separate paths after their unification, the struggle for independence had a similar pattern of development in each country. The French Revolution and the later influence of German Romanticism gave the Balkan peoples an ideology for revolt and a clear concept of the nation. In each country, the revolutionary movement was preceded and accompanied by a literary and cultural awakening. Freedom, in almost every instance, was attained with the aid of the Russian armies. Once liberated, each nation established a government based on the example of the Western constitutional monarchies. Each concentrated less on internal development than on the extension of its boundaries. The regimes set up became, despite their Western liberal form, parodies of popular government.

In the literary and cultural revival which preceded the political and military actions, each national group turned for inspiration to its own history: the Greeks, to ancient Greece and Byzantium; the Rumanians, to Rome; the Serbs and Bulgars, to their medieval empires. Great interest was shown in folk songs and legends and in the study of language. Having the strongest cultural tradition, the Greeks had been able to maintain a degree of educational and literary activity within the Orthodox Church throughout the Turkish occupation. In the literary revival of the eighteenth century, they turned to other aspects of national life. The works of both Rhigas Pheraios and Adamantios Korais emphasized the pagan classic tradition and the spirit of ancient rather than Byzantine Greece. Rhigas himself became an active revolutionary and fought for Greek freedom.

The Serbian literary revival was led by Dositej Obradović and Vuk Stefanović Karadžić. Particularly significant was their influence on the development of the literary language. In compiling a Serbian grammar and dictionary, Karadžić chose the Hercegovinian, or što, dialect as the purest and the best. This subsequently became the standard literary language. At the same time, the Croats, under the influence of Ljudevit Gaj, also accepted this dialect for their written language. The formulation and general acceptance of a standard language by both the Croats and the Serbs greatly facilitated the national movement and was the strongest basis for the later Yugoslav idea.

Unlike the Greeks and the Serbs, both the Rumanians and the Bulgarians had to contend with a strong foreign influence on their cultural life. In Rumania, the first literary language in use under Turkish domination had been Church Slavonic, but in the eighteenth century Greek became the language of education and government. At the end of this period, the Greek officials as well as the Rumanians were greatly influenced by the French political and cultural tradition. The French tie also contributed to the emphasis which the Rumanians now put on their Roman past—a heritage they shared with the French—and to their desire to favor those elements in their language which derived from Roman, rather than Slavic or Greek, roots. This relationship to France remained constant: French became the second language of educated Rumanians, and it was France which offered the principal support in the final stages of Rumanian unification.

The Bulgarian literary awakening encountered the greatest difficulties. With the economic revival in the Balkans, the Bulgarians —like the Greeks—found a wider world open to them. A middle class of merchants and teachers developed which was strongly influenced by the national and revolutionary ideas of the time. The first task of this group was to arouse the national feeling of the Bulgarians and to encourage them to fight to end both Turkish political domination and the Greek cultural control which was exercised through the church and the schools. The first important book in Bulgaria was written by a monk at Mt. Athos: Paisii. His history of Bulgaria, which was completed in 1762, was strongly nationalistic in tone and against Greek ecclesiastical control. The first printed book did not appear until 1806, when Bishop Sofronii published the *Kriakodromion* in Wallachia. In 1835 the first schools in which the instruction was in the Bulgarian language were opened and thereafter the educational facilities of the country developed quickly. The connection between national liberation and the freeing of education and religion from Greek dominance was thus established early.

National Revolt

SERBIA. Although the cultural revival occurred almost simultaneously in all the Balkan lands, it was in Serbia that the first successful revolt was staged. The rising of 1804 was intended as a protest against the gross maladministration and the oppressive acts of the local Turkish officials and the Janissaries rather than as an attempt to gain independence. The leader of the uprising was a pig merchant, Karadjordje. The revolt was successful at first and its leaders appealed to St. Petersburg for aid. The international situation proved to be unfavorable; the Russian government, involved in the struggle with Napoleon, advised caution. By 1806 the Ottoman government, worried by the progress of the revolt, offered to grant autonomy to Serbia. Meanwhile, however, the Serbs had been able to gain an alliance with Russia, herself at war with the Ottoman Empire, and they now demanded complete independence. Unfortunately for the Serbs, Russia proved to be an unreliable ally. After a defeat by the French, Tsar Alexander I met with Napoleon and concluded the Treaty of Tilsit in 1807. This agreement was followed by the commencement of peace negotiations with the Ottoman Empire. Left alone to face Turkish vengeance, the Serbs nevertheless continued to fight until 1813, when they met final defeat. The first Serbian revolution was thus crushed. Its chief weakness had been the failure to secure effective foreign, in particular Russian, assistance.

The Turks, in reoccupying the country, carried out such violent retaliatory measures that the Serbs again rebelled in 1815. This second revolution was led by Miloš Obrenović. The general international situation had now taken a much more favorable turn. France had been defeated and Russia had emerged as the dominant military and political power in eastern Europe. Fearing Russian intervention, the sultan granted Serbia autonomy, allowed it its own assembly (the Skupština), and recognized Miloš as prince of the pashalik of Belgrade. The Ottoman Empire continued to levy a tribute on the Serbs and to occupy certain fortresses in Serbia. These rights were reconfirmed in the Treaty of Akkerman (1826) and the Treaty of Adrianople (1829). Thus the second Serbian revolution ended in victory chiefly because this time Russian interests coincided with those of the Balkan state.

GREECE. The Serbian revolt, carried out in a remote section of Europe, had no significant international repercussions; the second Balkan revolution, that of the Greeks, dominated the diplomacy of the period. Of all of the Balkan peoples, the Greeks certainly were the best prepared to assert their independence because of their position within the Ottoman Empire. Their uprising was organized principally within the ranks of the merchant class. The center for the revolutionary activities was the port city of Odessa, where the *Philike Hetaeria* (Society of Friends) raised money and prepared for action. Once again, Russian influence was important. At first the leadership of the movement was offered to John Capodistrias, a Greek from Corfu who was the Russian foreign minister. When he refused, another Greek in the service of the tsar, General Alexander Ypsilanti, was chosen. The revolutionaries counted on Russian support. In March 1821 Ypsilanti led Greek troops over the Russian frontier into Moldavia; simultaneously a revolt broke out in the Morea. The main effort in the Rumanian principalities soon met with disaster, partly because of the animosity between Greek and Rumanian which had developed during the years of Phanariote rule. A Rumanian national revolt, under the leadership of Tudor Vladimirescu, had broken out at the same time and the two movements soon came into conflict. The Greeks seized and executed Vladimirescu and were in turn massacred by the Turkish forces. The revolt in the Morea, in contrast to that in the Principalities, continued.

The Greek revolution placed all the European powers in a difficult position. Because his political principles caused him to reject the idea of revolution against a legitimate government, Alexander I refused to aid the rebels, even when the Ottoman government hanged the Patriarch of Constantinople and a number of his followers. Capodistrias, who was naturally sympathetic to the Greek cause, was dismissed from office. It was thus apparent that Russia, despite her past traditions, would not come to the aid of Balkan Orthodox Christianity. Although little outside assistance was given to the rebels, the Turks could not crush the revolt on the Greek mainland. They were able, in general, to hold the large centers of population, but they could not follow the Greek insurgents into the mountains.

Despite the indifference of the governments, the Greek revolution evoked tremendous popular sympathy. The great movement of Philhellenism that swept over Europe inspired many to come to Greece to fight for the Greek cause. Particularly important was the participation of the poet, Byron, who died during the seige of Missolonghi in 1824. The enthusiastic popular reaction to what was considered the heroic struggle of a brave and ancient people against a cruel tyrant, together with fears of Russian moves, slowly influenced the British government. In 1823, in the first action taken by a foreign state to aid the revolt, London recognized the Greeks as belligerents.

The decisive factor in bringing about foreign intervention, however, occurred in 1825, when the Ottoman government summoned the powerful pasha of Egypt, Mohammed Ali, to assist in the subjugation of Greece. This ruler, although in theory a subject of the sultan, had with French assistance built a strong state and now rivaled his overlord in power. The sultan offered him both the island of Crete and the Morea if he were successful in suppressing the revolt. Because neither the British nor the Russians wished Egypt to dominate the eastern Mediterranean, the two governments now cooperated. Alexander I had been succeeded, in 1825, by the more energetic Nicholas I. In 1826 Russia and Britain signed an agreement to secure an autonomous Greece. In 1827 France joined these two powers in the Treaty of London, which had a similar aim. Meanwhile, relations between Russia and the Ottoman Empire deteriorated. Russia did not wish to become involved in a war for the sake of Greece, but she was concerned over the conditions in Rumania and Serbia, where the Turks were not fulfilling the obligations assumed under earlier treaties. In 1826 the Russian government and the Porte signed a new agreement, the Treaty of Akkerman, which reaffirmed previous pacts. Nevertheless, war between Russia and the Ottoman Empire did finally break out, largely because of the consequences of a dramatic naval encounter. In 1827 a joint French, British, and Russian fleet, which was patrolling Greek waters to check Mohammed Ali, became engaged in battle with the Turkish and Egyptian fleets and sank them. Enraged by this action, the Ottoman government rashly denounced the Treaty of Akkerman and the Russo-Turkish War of 1828 commenced.

In the period 1815-1914, the Balkan area witnessed four major wars: the Russo-Turkish War of 1828-29, the Crimean War of 1853-56, the Russo-Turkish War of 1877-78, and the Balkan Wars of 1912-13. Each of these conflicts brought about a series of major changes in the peninsula. In the Russo-Turkish War of 1828 the Russian armies marched through the Principalities, through the Balkan mountains, and after a hard campaign reached within striking distance of Constantinople. Here, in the city of Adrianople, the treaty of 1829 was signed. Its terms reaffirmed Serbian autonomy, placed the Rumanian Principalities under direct Russian protectorship, and established Greece as an autonomous tributary state.

The final form of the Greek state was set forth in the London Protocol of 1830 and in another agreement reached in 1832. In these pacts, France, Russia, and Britain agreed that independent Greece should be a monarchy and that Otto, the second son of the king of Bavaria, should be its first ruler. Although the powers had thus supported the cause of a free Greece, they were prepared to go only so far in changing political conditions in the Balkans. As a result, Greece at first was a small kingdom of 800,000 inhabitants—only one fourth of the Greek people of the Balkans. Thereafter successive Greek governments devoted their main energies to gaining the incorporation of the remaining Greek-inhabited territories.

Therefore, by 1832, despite the general desire for a respite after the Napoleonic Wars and the universal fear of revolutionary activity, Balkan nationalism had made great gains. Serbian autonomy had been recognized; an independent Greek kingdom had been established; and the Rumanian principalities had achieved a greater autonomy under Russian protection. Each of these states, however, contained within their boundaries only part of the national population. Most Greeks and Serbs still lived under Ottoman rule; a third of the Rumanian population lived in Transylvania, which was part of the Habsburg Empire. These revolutions were, therefore, only the first stages in the formation of the national states.

From 1832 to 1853, the year in which the Crimean War began, the chief dispute among the great powers involved the Egyptian threat to the integrity of the Ottoman Empire. At this time the British government was able to persuade the Ottoman Empire to issue its first major reform decree. In 1839 Sultan Abdul Mejid issued the Hatti-Sherif of the Gulhane (the Decree of the Rose Garden), in which all Ottoman citizens, Christian and Moslem alike, were guaranteed per-

THE BALKANS IN 1830 (after the Treaty of Adrianople)

sonal security and equality of taxation. The conditions of military service were also to be reformed. The British government hoped that reform within the empire would make the state acceptable to all its subjects and that it would remain as a bulwark against Russian expansion. Unfortunately for the later fate of the Ottoman Empire, the reforms were unsuccessful.

The Crimean War

The series of events which led to the outbreak of the Crimean War commenced with a quarrel between Orthodox and Catholics over religious issues, which involved Russia and France, the respective patrons of these churches in the Ottoman Empire. The basis of conflict shifted when the Russian government demanded what was, in effect, the recognition of its protectorship over the Balkan Orthodox Christians. The war, which was preceded by long negotiations, was finally waged because of British fears of Russian predominance in Constantinople and the Russian inability to control the diplomatic situation. In 1854 French and British troops landed in the Crimea, where, after a difficult campaign, they were finally able to capture the fortress of Sevastopol. This victory, together with the Austrian threat to enter the war if peace were not concluded, forced Russia to accept the Treaty of Paris of 1856. Under the terms of the agreement, Russia abandoned many of the advantages which she had enjoyed in the Balkans since the Treaty of Kuchuk Kainardji. First, she agreed to the demilitarization and neutralization of the Black Sea. This measure protected the British maritime position in the eastern Mediterranean and eliminated the Russian naval threat to Constantinople. Second, Russia abandoned her claim to the exclusive protectorship over the Balkan Christians and agreed that this role would be assumed jointly by the great powers. This stipulation proved to be largely meaningless; Russia continued thereafter as the chief patron of Balkan nationalism, but she could no longer claim the right to intervene in Turkish affairs on the basis of international agreements. Third, southern Bessarabia was returned to Moldavia. Fourth, the Russian protectorate over the Danubian Principalities and Serbia was replaced by a collective guarantee.

The Treaty of Paris, which marked an enormous loss of Russian prestige, proved to be more significant for central Europe and Italy than for the Balkan peninsula. It did, however, cause a change in Russian foreign policy which also affected the Balkans. The Russian government, after the military disaster it had suffered in the Crimea, realized that it would have to concentrate on reforming and strengthening of the Russian state. In the 1860s a series of reforms were introduced, the most important of which was the abolition of serfdom. Because of this concentration on internal affairs, a policy of virtual withdrawal from international events was adopted. As a result, for the next twenty years the Balkans experienced no major international crises involving all the great powers. European diplomacy now concentrated its attention on central Europe and on the events connected with the unification of Germany and Italy.

After the Crimean War, the British government, in pursuance of its policy of supporting the maintenance of the Ottoman Empire, urged the Porte to issue a second reform decree, the Hatti-Humayun of 1856. In this document the religious and legal equality of the Christians in the empire was again guaranteed. But, like the earlier reform proposals, this decree was also largely ineffective.

The Formation of Rumania

The principal event in the Balkans immediately after the Crimean War was the unification of the Danubian Principalities to form the modern Rumanian state. This action, in contrast to the national movements of the other Balkan states, was accomplished through diplomacy and without bloodshed. Throughout the period of Ottoman domination Moldavia and Wallachia had enjoyed a theoretical autonomy. Their position between St. Petersburg and Constantinople gave them a great strategic value. Russian interest in the region commenced during the reign of Peter the Great. At that time the two provinces lost their right to chose their own princes because of the aid they had given the Russian tsar. In 1774, in the Treaty of Kuchuk Kainardji, Russia expressed her concern over the affairs of the Principalities and her right to intervene in their behalf. In 1812, when Russia took the Moldavian province of Bessarabia, the foundation for later conflict was laid.

Russian influence in the affairs of the Principalities remained strong in the years following the Congress of Vienna. After the Russo-Turkish War of 1828-29, the Treaty of Adrianople established the Principalities as Russian protectorates. In the next years, with the Russian armies in occupation, a reorganization of the government was undertaken. In two sets of administrative statutes, the Organic Regulations, each Principality was provided with separate but parallel institutions. Each was to have a governor (*hospodar*) and an assembly of landowners (*boyars*). In the years of the protectorate, Russia, through her consuls in Jassy and Bucharest, exercised a supervisory function and interfered repeatedly in the internal affairs of the Principalities. Russian control favored the interests of the great conservative landowners and brought opposition on the part of the liberals, who also drew their members from the privileged classes. In 1848 a revolution broke out. The leaders of the revolt wished to be rid of Russian influence as well as of Turkish sovereignty. Russian armies suppressed the movement.

Despite the fact that Russia held a protectorate over the country and that her influence did aid certain groups in the population, most Rumanian political leaders looked to France for inspiration and assistance. And it was indeed France and her ruler, Napoleon III, that were principally responsible for the unification of the Principalities. During the peace conference following the Crimean War, France supported the desires of the Rumanians, who wished to unite the two provinces into a single state. This action was opposed by Britain, which did not wish the Ottoman Empire to be further weakened, and by Austria, which did not want a strong state to be created on the lower Danube. Because no agreement could be reached at the conference, it was decided that the wishes of the population should first be ascertained. In the three successive elections held to choose members to the assemblies in the next years, it soon became apparent that the overwhelming desire was for union. In the last election, held in the winter of 1858-59, the Rumanians were able to circumvent the prohibition on union by electing the same man, Alexander Cuza, as governor in both Principalities. This measure succeeded largely because the major powers were deeply involved in the question of Italian unification. Neither Britain, Turkey, nor Austria could act. France favored unification and Russia supported her. The recognition of Cuza as governor of both Principalities did not signify the real unification of the country. It was not until 1861 that Cuza was able to combine the administrative systems of the two provinces and to declare the creation of the Rumanian state.

After the union of Moldavia and Wallachia, two major territorial problems remained. Although Moldavia had reacquired southern Bessarabia after the Crimean War, it was clear that Russia would not regard this cession as final. Equally important, a large Rumanian population in Transylvania remained under Habsburg control.

United Rumania thus had unresolved territorial issues with both her great neighbors.

The Formation of Bulgaria

Bulgaria was the fourth of the Balkan states to gain its freedom. The first step toward national liberation had been the Bulgarian literary and educational revival. The second step, now necessary, was the freeing of the Bulgarian Orthodox Church from Greek influence. In 1870, with Russian diplomatic assistance, a Bulgarian Exarchate was established—a move which gave the Bulgarians their own ecclesiastical organization. Not only did the Exarchate receive jurisdiction over some seventeen Bulgarian districts, but its control could be extended over any neighboring diocese in which two thirds of the people voted for it. This provision was to be particularly significant in the struggle over Macedonia.

The opportunity for revolt came when a rebellion against Ottoman rule broke out in Hercegovina in 1875. The great powers attempted to calm the situation and to suggest reforms, but by the summer of 1876 both Serbia and Montenegro were at war with the Ottoman Empire. The revolt of these Orthodox Slavic peoples was received with great sympathy in Russia, particularly in Panslav circles. Although Panslavism took different forms, most of its adherents believed that Russia should assume the leadership of the Slavic peoples and work for the eventual unification of Orthodox Slavic nations. This program thus involved conflict not only with the Ottoman Empire, but also with the Habsburg monarchy. Although the Russian foreign office consistently resisted Panslav pressure, its position was difficult because many influential Russians did subscribe to these doctrines. Panslav support of the Balkan revolutionaries and the popular desire for Russian intervention became stronger when Turkish atrocities in Bulgaria resulted in some 10,000 to 15,000 deaths. The "Bulgarian Horrors," as they were known in Britain, stirred public opinion both in Russia and in Britain.

Meanwhile, the war did not go well for the Balkan Slavs. When Serbia was defeated, and forced to accept an armistice with the Ottoman Empire, the Russian government turned to the aid of the Bulgarians, who were still in revolt. In preparation for a possible war with the Ottoman Empire, Russia first made an agreement with the Habsburg Empire, which promised to remain netural in return for the guarantee of future gains in Bosnia-Hercegovina and the assurance that no large Slavic state would be formed. Finally, in 1877, the third conflict between Russia and Turkey since the Congress of Vienna broke out. Again, after a difficult military campaign, Russia forced the Ottoman Empire to sign a treaty surrendering rights and territories. The most important provisions of the Treaty of San Stefano (1878) called for the creation of a great Bulgarian state, which included most of Macedonia. Although the boundaries established were not in gross violation of the national principle, the erection of a large Bulgaria would have completely upset the balance of power in the Balkans. Both Britain and Austria expected any Bulgarian state to be little more than a Russian puppet. The treaty was also a violation of Russia's prewar agreement with the Habsburg Empire that no great state would be created. A period of acute tension followed, but Russia finally agreed to come to the Congress of Berlin (1878) and submit to a revision of the Treaty of San Stefano.

The Treaty of Berlin, the most important single agreement for the Balkan states in the nineteenth century, divided the new Bulgaria into three sections. Only one of these, Bulgaria, was given a separate, autonomous existence. A second part, Eastern Rumelia, was placed under a Christian governor and remained in a semiautonomous position within the Ottoman Empire. The third part, Macedonia, was returned to direct Turkish rule. Serbia, Montenegro, and Rumania were recognized as independent, not autonomous, states. All received territorial increases. Serbia extended her boundary southward; Rumania received Dobrudja; Montenegro was doubled in size. In subsequent negotiations, Greece received Thessaly and a part of Epirus. The great powers also made gains. Austria was given the right to occupy and to administer Bosnia-Hercegovina; Russia again took southern Bessarabia from Rumania. Britain acquired the island of Cyprus from the Ottoman Empire as compensation for Russian acquisitions in the Caucasus. The settlement satisfied no one (with the possible exception of Great Britain). The Bulgarians were the most disappointed. In subsequent years the restoration of the boundaries established in the Treaty of San Stefano, which largely coincided with those of medieval Bulgaria, became the goal of every Bulgarian nationalist.

At the Congress of Berlin the powers recognized that Russia would be the predominant power in Bulgaria. The Russian authorities now supervised the organization of a new government, as they had previously done in the Rumanian Principalities. Under Russian direction the Bulgarians drew up and adopted a liberal constitution. Their first ruler, endorsed by Russia, was Alexander of Battenberg, a German prince and a nephew of the tsar. Despite their favorable commencement, relations between Bulgaria and Russia soon grew strained because both Alexander and the Bulgarian political leaders came to resent Russian interference in their internal affairs. In 1885 the province of Eastern Rumelia revolted and declared itself a part of Bulgaria. Against the express wishes of Russia, Alexander of Battenberg accepted the leadership of the national movement. In an attempt to gain compensation, Serbia then declared war on Bulgaria. The subsequent military triumph of Bulgaria over the Serbian armies made the union of Eastern Rumelia and Bulgaria inevitable. No power was now willing to hinder its accomplishment.

In 1886 the supporters of Russia, who now favored Alexander's replacement, kidnapped the prince and engineered a *coup* in Sofia. Although the revolutionary government was subsequently overthrown, Alexander was forced to abdicate. The removal of the prince did not result in a restoration of Russian influence. A complete break in diplomatic relations between the two countries occurred in 1886. In 1887, in the face of strong Russian protests, the Bulgarians proceeded to elect another prince, Ferdinand of Coburg. Austrian and British fears that Bulgaria would be nothing but a Russian colony were thus not justified by the events. As it had in Rumania, the Russian protectorship in Bulgaria lost St. Petersburg the sympathy and support of the national leadership.

The Congress of Berlin marked the close of the first stage of Balkan national liberation. Four states—Serbia, Greece, Rumania, and Bulgaria—were established. Because each of these had further territorial aims, the next step in Balkan development was the concentration on the acquisition of new lands. In almost every instance, however, the territories remaining under foreign rule were claimed by one or more of the Balkan states. Thus the success of the national individual movements in fact considerably increased the antagonism and hostility between the Balkan peoples.

The Internal Development of the Balkan States

The political and social development of the new states proved a disappointment to those who had expected that the abolition of Turkish rule would be followed by a sudden regeneration of national life. Although certain improvements were indeed immediately evi-

THE BALKANS IN 1878

dent, there was no general upsurge. The daily life of the vast majority of the population was, as late as the 1930s, much what it had been on the day of national liberation. In some instances, conditions actually declined. The responsibility for this situation lay in the general social and economic situation and in the quality of the political leadership in the Balkan states.

In each of the Balkan nations the revolution against Ottoman rule was led by the predominant class within the Christian community. In Rumania the leadership naturally fell to the landowner, who was usually educated abroad and kept in close touch with Western culture. In Greece the merchant class, with its wealth and wide experience abroad, and the local notables in the villages of the mainland provided the leadership for revolt. In Serbia and Bulgaria, which lacked a native aristocracy or a large commercial class, political power lay generally in the hands of what may be termed the Balkan middle class of merchants, intellectuals, well-to-do landowners, and professional men. In their struggle against the Ottoman Empire, the chief desire of all these groups was simply liberation from foreign control. They accepted generally the political concepts associated with the French Revolution and European liberalism. Once national independence had been won, however, it was not the local leaders but the great powers who determined the form of government. Principally concerned with establishing stable governments that would insure the peace, the great powers preferred that the newly liberated countries have strong executives and—except in the case of Serbia—they placed foreign (that is, German) princes on the new thrones. Constitutional governments were thus established, but under monarchs of another nationality and usually from courts with a strong autocratic tradition. The Balkan monarchs all expected to rule their kingdoms; few had great sympathy for constitutional limitations.

The constitutions with which the states were endowed usually contained guarantees of personal liberty and promised wide suffrage and universal participation in affairs of state. In practice, this constitutional façade hid governments which little resembled the regimes in England, Belgium, the United States, and the Scandinavian countries —ostensibly the models upon which the Balkan systems were based. The real power in the state was held by a relatively small group of politicians who generally surrounded and worked with the ruler. In most instances those who had led the national struggle used the victory to secure their own personal advancement and wealth.

The lack of experience in self-government caused by the centuries of foreign rule led, as might have been expected, to many difficulties. The Christian bureaucrat's attitude toward public office too often resembled that of the Ottoman official whose activities he had once so strongly denounced. He had, after all, no other model of behavior. The corruption of the Ottoman period was thus carried over into the national era.

At the time of their liberation from Turkish rule, all the Balkan states were primitive and poor. Rumania, with her enormous resources in grain and minerals, was in the best position. The real need of each nation was for a period of peace and concentration on internal improvements and education. Instead, the primary interest of every Balkan government became the acquisition of more territory and the liberation of those of its nationals still under foreign rule. Although this goal is understandable under the conditions of the time, it often had quite unfortunate results. The lands still under Ottoman domination were mixed in nationality and the claims of the Balkan states overlapped. Further moves against the Ottoman Empire thus tended to increase tension and rivalry among the Balkan peoples. Moreover, this concentration on foreign-policy objectives required the maintenance of a strong army and police force. The goal of national aggrandizement thus not only diverted money from internal needs but also resulted in the creation and maintenance of a military establishment which could make or break the government itself. The emphasis on national expansion and the consequent importance of the armies thus explains much of the lack of economic development in the Balkans and also the political instability of most of the governments.

SERBIA. Although Serbia was not given a foreign ruler, her situation was probably even less favorable than that of her neighbors because the throne was disputed by not one, but two, national dynasties. Serbia's political history is the most turbulent of that of any Balkan country in the nineteenth century; there were eight changes of rulers between 1815 and 1903. Although the original Serbian uprising was led by Karadjordje; it was Miloš Obrenović who became the first prince of Serbia. This ruler then had his rival assassinated, and the ensuing feud between the Karadjordjević and Obrenović families lasted until 1903. The government established by Miloš was well suited to the condition of the country—a land of small peasant holdings. It was patriarchal in character and the national assembly played but a small role. In 1838 Miloš was forced to grant a constitution which gave a great deal of power to a senate, the members of which were appointed for life. In 1839 he abdicated in favor of his son, Milan, who died almost at once. He was succeeded by his brother, Michael. In 1842 Michael was replaced by Alexander Karadjordjević (1842-58). During his reign the real power lay in the hands of the senators. In 1844 the Austrian civil code was introduced, reinforcing the trend toward centralization; henceforth, local government was to play a less important role in Serbia. In 1858 Alexander was deposed and Miloš Obrenović was recalled to the throne, to be followed once more, in 1860, by Michael Obrenović. In 1861 a new constitution was drawn up which increased the power of the ruler. In this period, too, the last of the Turkish garrisons was removed from Serbia. Michael's assassination in 1868 brought to power his cousin, Milan Obrenovič, whose reign was notable for its foreign policy and for the change which it brought in the political alignment of the country. As has been mentioned, Serbia suffered a grave military defeat in 1876, when she went to war with the Ottoman Empire. Russia, once a firm supporter of Serbian aspirations, thereafter turned her attention almost exclusively to securing Bulgarian claims. Serbia was thus forced to turn to the Habsburg monarchy—a move which was extremely unpopular with the usually pro-Russian Serbs. The change coincided with the Austrian occupation of Bosnia-Hercegovina, which had been agreed upon at the Congress of Berlin. These provinces, inhabited by South Slavs of both Serb and Croat extraction, were part of the unredeemed territory Serbia wished to absorb. Although Serbia did obtain Niš and other lands to the south with Austrian support, these gains did not compensate for the loss of the more important provinces. In addition, Milan signed secret political and commercial treaties with Vienna (1881) which made Serbia, in fact, a vassal of the Danubian monarchy. This unpopular policy was difficult to maintain, but there appeared to be no real alternative to alignment with Vienna. Finally, in 1885 Milan made the enormous error of launching an attack on Bulgaria at the time of her unification with Eastern Rumelia. His humiliating defeat forced him to accept a new constitution in 1888, and then to abdicate and go into exile in 1889.

Milan's son, Alexander Obrenović, who succeeded him, proved an even less able ruler. As soon as he was of age he reinvoked the constitution of 1869 and recalled his father as an adviser. The royal family henceforth became a source of national scandal. Alexander's parents had already become notorious through their open and public quarreling. The new king now proceeded to deepen the wound to national pride caused by the conduct of the royal family by marrying a widow, Draga Mašina, who had a very dubious reputation and was unable to have children. The danger thus existed that the Obrenović dynasty would die out. In 1903 Alexander and his wife were assassinated in a particularly bloody *coup*, the details of which shocked the European public. As a result of this revolt, the sixty-year-old Peter Karadjordjević came to the throne. He proved a far more effective and popular ruler than Alexander. During his reign notable internal reforms were undertaken and an effective system of parliamentary government was instituted. The direction of the state's foreign policy also changed. Peter's pro-Russian and pro-French tendencies made it inevitable that the Austrian alignment could not be maintained. He not only severed the tie with Vienna, but he also embarked upon a new path which was bound to bring Serbia into conflict with Austria. The internal developments in Serbia had thus brought to power a man who was willing and eager to embark on a positive program of national expansion.

GREECE. The domestic scene in Greece presented a similar picture, although it lacked the rapid change of rulers that occurred in Serbia. In 1833 the Bavarian prince, Otto, who now became King Othon, arrived in Athens with a large retinue of Bavarian soldiers and advisers. He then tried to apply patterns of administration which had been developed in the well-ordered communities of central Europe to the small, war-ravaged Balkan state. Moreover, the real authority lay, not in his hands, but in those of the three powers—France, Britain, and Russia—which had established the country and had been designated its protectors by international treaty. Each of these states tried to influence and manipulate Greece's internal affairs in such a manner as to further its own general interests in the Mediterranean. The three main political parties in Greece were, in fact as well as in name, French, British, and Russian. This situation, which had no parallel in any other Balkan country, proved disastrous for the early years of Greek political life. The principal disputes were between the French and British parties. Britain wanted Greece to make no further moves to expand her national boundaries at the expense of the Ottoman Empire. France, with her own interests in Algeria and Egypt, had no such objections. France's willingness to encourage and accept Greek ambitions contributed to making her the most important power in Athens. Russia, excluded from real influence because of her lack of naval power in the Mediterranean, tried to use the Orthodox Church to further her interests in Greece.

The first decades of the modern Greek state were marked by foreign intervention, continual financial difficulties, and constant conflicts between the Bavarian ruler and the Greek politicians. In 1843 one of many financial crises led to a military *coup*, which was supported by the British and Russian parties. As a result of the revolt, the king agreed to a constitution. The document, drawn up in 1844 by a national constituent assembly, provided for an elected assembly and an appointed senate. The change to a constitutional monarchy, however, had little effect on the actual governing of the country. The king now ruled through ministers who, in turn, managed the elections. The French party of Kolettis remained in power and was able to win great popular support through its constant emphasis on national expansion. Kolettis is closely associated with the development of the Great Idea, or *Megale Idea*, a policy which called for the unification of all the Greeks. An extreme interpretation of this concept signified the recreation of the Byzantine Empire. The chief opponent to Greek expansion remained Great Britain, which used her naval supremacy to exert influence on Athens. In 1862 another military *coup* forced Othon to abdicate. In the negotiations between the powers that followed, the British—using the promise to give the Ionian Islands to Greece—were able to place on the throne a candidate of their choice, William of Glücksburg, who became George I (1863-1913). In 1864 a more democratic constitution was adopted which introduced the principle of universal male suffrage.

The question of the unredeemed lands also dominated the long reign of the new king. Political life at the end of the century was marked by the rivalry of two politicians: Charilaos Trikoupes, who wished to adopt a policy of internal development and moderation abroad, and Theodore Deligiannes, who favored concentration on international questions. The establishment of the Bulgarian state and, later, its union with Eastern Rumelia, was regarded as detrimental to Greek interests because of the conflicting claims to Macedonia. The Greeks were also disappointed with the results of the Congress of Berlin. Although they had received Thessaly and a part of Epirus in 1881, they had wished for more. In addition, Britain, in order to improve her strategic position in the eastern Mediterranean, had taken the island of Cyprus, which was inhabited by a majority of Greeks.

Another crisis of the Greek national movement occurred at the end of the century. There had been repeated revolts on the Turkish-held island of Crete in the nineteenth century. Each was doomed to failure by British opposition to a change in the status of the island. In 1896 another such rebellion took place; the Cretans again called for union with Greece. Greek volunteers flocked to the island, and, in 1897, the Greek government went to war with Turkey. This move proved a disaster; the Turkish armies, recently reorganized, invaded Greek territory and only the intervention of the great powers saved the country. Despite the Greek military defeat, the Cretans won autonomy. A government under a Greek prince was set up—an arrangement that made almost inevitable the eventual annexation of the island by Greece.

Military defeat and the financial burden it involved brought Greece into bankruptcy and forced her to accept a further degree of foreign control. As the internal situation deteriorated, Eleutherios Venizelos, the greatest statesman of modern Greece, assumed power. Under his influence a new constitution was drawn up in 1911 and a reform of the civil and military establishment was undertaken. He subsequently came to dominate Greek internal politics and was successful in obtaining further territory for his country.

RUMANIA. The third state to be united, Rumania, presented a much calmer political picture. Prince Cuza, who had led the struggle for the unification of the country, was not an aggressive or active man. Nevertheless, he did introduce two great reforms. The first was the confiscation of the lands of the Dedicated Monasteries. These religious establishments, usually administered by Greek officials, owned about a quarter of the land in Wallachia and a third of that in Moldavia. The income from these estates was "dedicated" to the upkeep of certain holy places, such as the monasteries on Mount Athos, which were also under Greek control. When the monks refused to negotiate on the question of compensation, Cuza simply appropriated the land. The second measure, the agrarian law of 1864, corresponded to similar measures being carried out in Russia at the same time. The peasants were freed from their obligations to their local lords and given small plots of their own. Although, in theory, this reform freed the peasant from feudal obligations and should have improved his general position, the administration of the law— like that of the country itself—was in the hands of the large land-owners. In the next few years the position of the Rumanian peasant deteriorated sharply. The peasant who could not support himself from his own land was forced to work for the large landowner—and on the latter's terms. With the great demand for Rumanian wheat in European markets, it was to the advantage of the large producer to acquire as much land as possible and to introduce machines. This increased the pressure on the peasant and also raised the price of land. The laws on agricultural contracts, passed in 1866 and 1872, operated to the great disadvantage of the small peasant and of agricultural labor in general. The pattern of Rumanian society, unlike that of neighboring Serbia and Bulgaria, still placed the large land-owner in a predominant position. The peasant, although free in theory, was often actually not in a better condition than he had been before.

Cuza also introduced reforms in education and modeled the judicial system of his country after that of France. His measures naturally aroused much opposition. In 1866 a military *coup* forced his withdrawal, and now Rumania too obtained a foreign prince. Charles of Hohenzollern-Sigmaringen, the new ruler, was moderate and conciliatory. A constitution, based on that of Belgium, was introduced; but despite its democratic form, the government of Rumania remained in the hands of a privileged minority. Of the two parties competing for political power, the Conservatives represented the interests of the large landowners and the Liberals supported the interests of the middle classes and the smaller landowners.

As in Greece and Serbia, foreign affairs played a major role in Rumanian politics. The largest number of Rumanians outside the state lived in neighboring Transylvania. This district, however, was under the control of a great power, the Habsburg Empire, and the chances of its acquisition by Rumania seemed slight. Because Russia had taken southern Bessarabia in 1878 and offered in compensation the poorer Bulgarian territory of Dobrudja, Rumania allied with Austria and Germany in 1883. This alignment was never popular, for Rumanian sympathies were consistently pro-French.

Political life in Rumania, as in the other Balkan states, was characterized by corruption in public office. Conservative and Liberal candidates alternated in office, but no real changes in public life were effected. In 1907 a great peasant revolt shook the country. Although the army succeeded in crushing it, the rebellion brought to light the bad conditions in the countryside. Once again reforms were introduced, but they were still administered to the benefit of the large landowner.

BULGARIA. United in 1885, Bulgaria had only a relatively short national history before the outbreak of World War I. The successor of Alexander of Battenberg, who was forced out by Russian pressure, was Ferdinand of Coburg, who ruled until 1918. During the first years of his reign, the country was governed by the leading Bulgarian statesman of the era, Stefan Stambulov. It was he who had directed the policy of defiance of Russia. This attitude toward St. Petersburg was very difficult and dangerous for Bulgaria to maintain, because no other European power could be counted on for assistance. The situation became more difficult when Ferdinand married an Italian princess and had his son baptized in the Roman Catholic Church. This move greatly antagonized Russia, the patron of Balkan Orthodoxy. Ferdinand, however, who wished to rule himself, soon came into conflict with his strong-willed minister. It was also recognized that the maintenance of a policy of opposition to Russia would put Bulgaria at a great disadvantage in international relations. In 1894 Stambulov was forced out of office; in 1895 he was assassinated while the police "looked the other way." Ferdinand thereafter sought a reconciliation with Russia and in 1896 relations between the two countries were brought back to normal. Despite the resumption of diplomatic ties, Russia did not take up again her once-ardent support of Bulgarian claims and she no longer supported the re-establishment of the greater Bulgaria of the Treaty of San Stefano.

Under Ferdinand's administration, conditions in Bulgaria rapidly improved. Foreign observers were, in general, greatly impressed by the new spirit in what had once been the most exploited of the Ottoman European provinces. Nevertheless, the same abuses that marred the record of other Balkan governments made their appearance in Bulgaria also. Great progress was made in the development of schools, roads, and the army, but these were accompanied by the same graft and corruption to be found elsewhere in the Balkans. Moreover, the desire to acquire further lands in Macedonia soon dominated all other political issues. It was this question which was to lead Bulgaria to support the losing side in three consecutive wars.

MACEDONIA. In the years immediately preceding World War I, the area most disputed by the Balkan states was the last major piece of Turkish-held territory in Europe: Macedonia. The conflicting claims of Bulgaria, Serbia, and Greece had been established far back in their national history. A land of relatively little economic value, Macedonia had about three million inhabitants in 1900. The majority of them were Slavs, but there was a strong minority of Greeks, Albanians, Turks, and Kutzo-Vlachs. The principal problem was the national allegiance of the Slavs, most of whom spoke local dialects closely akin to Bulgarian. Nationality in Europe has traditionally been determined by language, but in Macedonia the question of language itself was controversial. On the one hand, it was possible to regard the people of the territory as Macedonians, and their dialects as a separate Macedonian language. On the other hand, it could be argued that the territory of Macedonia was inhabited by Serbians, Bulgarians, and Greeks. It was easy to distinguish the Greek-speaking minority but, because the Serbian and Bulgarian languages are closely related, it was difficult to separate Serb from Bulgar. If the inhabitants were to be regarded as Macedonian, then a good argument could be made for the establishment of an independent state; if, however, they belonged to the three separate nationalities, partition was the obvious solution—but a problem remained: where was the boundary to be drawn? The Greeks, a minority in the area, sought to strengthen their claims by arguing that it was possible to speak a Slavic language yet feel oneself to be Greek. As a result of this conflict of claims and confusion of principle, the unfortunate inhabitants of Macedonia found themselves the objects of intensive propaganda designed to convince them that they were of one nationality rather than of another. Each of the three states involved sponsored the formation of national societies within Macedonia and they waged a bitter campaign for predominance. When traditional methods of political propaganda failed, terror was freely employed. Each government assiduously collected statistics and drew up maps and charts to justify its claims. Aside from the national aspects and purely from a strategic standpoint, none of the nations involved could allow its opponents a full victory in the matter. The domination of Macedonia, because of its strategic position, would give its owner control of the peninsula. The tragedy of Macedonia thus lay not only in the disastrous effects which this conflict had upon the inhabitants, but also in the fact that it made political cooperation among Serbia, Bulgaria, and Greece almost impossible.

By 1903 the situation had become so bad that the European powers were forced to intervene. The decrepit Turkish administration did not have the force to confine the fierce conflict. In the Mürsteg agreement, Austria and Russia attempted to introduce reforms in Macedonia and to provide for foreign participation in their administration. These proposals, like similar proposed reforms in the Ottoman domains, were never carried out. The ultimate disposition of the land was finally determined by war, first by the Balkan states in alliance against the Ottoman Empire and then by a conflict between Bulgaria and her former allies.

After 1910, in order to halt what appeared to be an Austrian drive toward the Aegean, the Russian government attempted to establish a Balkan bloc. Under Russian sponsorship, Greece, Bulgaria, Serbia, and Montenegro came to an agreement in 1912, but instead of forming a front against Austrian penetration, the Balkan allies made plans to divide among themselves the rest of the Turkish territories in Europe. In October 1912 the First Balkan War began. Soon the Turkish armies were forced back until they held only Constantinople and the surrounding area. In the peace negotiations that followed, the former Balkan allies quarreled over the division of the territorial spoils. In the Second Balkan War of 1913, Bulgaria attempted to secure her claims by force and went to war with Greece, Serbia, Rumania, and Turkey. As a result of her subsequent defeat, Bulgaria lost the gains she had made in the First Balkan War with the exception of a strip of land which connected her territory with the Aegean port of Dedeagatch (Alexandropolis). She also lost Dobrudja to Rumania. Thus Bulgaria—far from achieving her national goal: the boundaries of San Stefano—received the smallest share of the division of Macedonia. The Macedonian issue thereafter divided Bulgaria from her neighbors and remained the principal question in Bulgarian foreign policy.

ALBANIA. The Balkan Wars, which resulted in the expulsion of Turkish power from Europe, also brought about the creation of the last of the modern Balkan states: Albania. Albanian nationalism had been late in awakening. Because approximately 70 per cent of the population was Moslem, the Albanians suffered less under Ottoman rule than did other Balkan peoples. Individual Albanians had played important roles in the administration of the empire and the country itself had enjoyed virtual self-government. Divided into three religious groups, the Albanians could find no point of unity in a common faith. Their education was under foreign influence. Greek was the language of the Orthodox Church and, therefore, of the education of the Orthodox population; the Moslems employed Turkish. No significant national literature existed until 1878, when for the first time the Albanians were allowed to open schools and to print books in their own language. In 1886 these were again banned. The strongest impulsion for the national movement thereafter came from Albanian emigrants in Italy and the United States.

National organization was finally forced upon the Albanians. In 1878 they were compelled to form a league to fight off the attempt of both Greece and Montenegro to take territory inhabited by clearly Albanian populations. They had no great desire to break away from the Ottoman Empire for they recognized that they were too weak to stand alone. The Young Turk Revolution of 1908, however, left them with no real alternative. This movement was the Turkish reaction to the territorial losses of the past and the diminishing prestige and power of the Ottoman Empire. The revolutionary group wished to reform and strengthen the Turkish government and to bring an end to the series of defeats it had suffered. At first the movement seemed to herald a national regeneration and to offer new hope for the empire. The Albanians were again allowed to open schools. Soon, however, the revolution turned in a narrowly nationalistic direction. Turkish was again made the language of education in Albania and other measures were taken which were so repressive in nature that they brought about revolts in 1910 and 1911. Thus, when the Balkan Wars commenced, the Albanians were ready to seek independence. They also feared that the alternative would be the partition of the country by Serbia and Greece.

The establishment of the modern Albanian state in 1913 resulted from the expulsion of Turkey from Europe after the Balkan Wars. Both the Habsburg Empire and Italy supported the Albanian movement because they did not wish Serbia to absorb the area or to acquire land on the Adriatic Sea. A German prince, William of Wied, became the first ruler of Albania, but World War I broke out before the boundaries of his state could be firmly established. Moreover, William was unable to establish a stable regime. After only six months in power, he was forced to flee the country. In 1914, therefore, Albania had neither settled frontiers nor an established government. She was not to have them until after the war.

The Yugoslav Movement and the Habsburg Empire

By 1914 the Balkan states had settled their claims on the Ottoman territories in Europe, although neither Greece, Bulgaria, nor Serbia were satisfied with their respective shares in the partition. With the Turkish question closed, attention turned to the Habsburg Empire, the state which now held the largest number of Balkan peoples under its rule. After the Treaty of Karlowitz (1699), the boundaries of the Habsburg Empire had advanced gradually as the Turkish armies were forced back. This process brought increasing numbers of Croats and Serbs into the Habsburg domains, where they joined the other peoples of the multinational empire. Although the Habsburg Empire had in many respects represented a supranational principle, the nineteenth and twentieth centuries were ages of nationalism. Like the Balkan peoples, the subjects of the Habsburg Empire began to discover their own national identities.

The national problem in the Danubian monarchy became particularly difficult after 1867. The 1860s brought about the unification of Germany and Italy, areas over which Austria had once exerted a large measure of control. Forced out of central Europe, Vienna could turn only southward. In the last quarter of the nineteenth century, the great states of Europe all pursued imperial policies. France, England, and Germany used their naval power to make conquests in Asia and Africa. Russia moved overland into China and Central Asia. Landbound Austria could expand only in the Balkans. Here, however, she met not only the opposition of other great powers, but also the difficulties which arose in connection with the reorganization of government she was forced to make after her defeat by Prussia.

Faced with the rise of national feeling among its subjects, the Habsburg government decided to come to terms with the strongest of the national groups: the Hungarians. In the *Ausgleich* (Compromise) of 1867, the empire was divided into the Austrian Empire and the Hungarian Kingdom. The Habsburg emperor, Franz Joseph, remained the ruler of the new Dual Monarchy. Foreign affairs, the military establishment, and financial affairs as related to these two domains were administered jointly, but in all other matters the two sections were separate.

In the division of the lands occupied by Balkan peoples, Dalmatia and Slovenia fell to Austria; Croatia, Slavonia, the Vojvodina, and Transylvania went to Hungary. Immediately after the *Ausgleich*, the Hungarian government made an agreement with the Croats which allowed them limited self-government. Unfortunately, the arrangement did not succeed and the following years brought about a rapid growth of antagonism and friction between the two peoples. The Hungarians, now in a strong position, proceeded to govern with little regard for the sensitivities of the national groups under them. A policy of Magyarization was embarked upon, which naturally provoked a fierce reaction. As a result, Hungarian rule over the South Slavic peoples set the scene for the great change that was to take place in their political status in 1918.

Although the chief national problem facing the empire involved the South Slavs, a word must also be said about Transylvania. This area had a majority of Rumanian inhabitants (55 per cent), but also strong German (8 per cent) and Hungarian (34 per cent) minorities. Although the process of Magyarization was resented in Transylvania, too, the national movement was not as strong there as it was in the Slavic sections of the empire, chiefly because it received little encouragement from the outside. Unlike Belgrade, Bucharest did not become a revolutionary center for the Rumanian national cause. After the loss of southern Bessarabia in 1878, Rumania allied herself with the German powers and her chief concern in foreign affairs remained her relations with Russia. It was evident that the annexation of Transylvania could be carried out only with the destruction of Austria-Hungary—which, in view of the power of Russia, would not be to the advantage of Rumania. It was clearly to her interest to maintain a balance of power between her great neighbors. Thus the Rumanians of Transylvania worked for reform and for an increase in their rights. They disliked Hungarian control and they hoped for assistance from Vienna in protecting their position.

The greatest danger to the integrity of the empire was thus posed by the South Slavs. Not only were their numbers large, but their cause was regarded with sympathy by Serbia, Montenegro, and Russia. It should be strongly emphasized that the national movements within the Habsburg Empire, with a few exceptions, did not at first seek the dissolution of the Dual Monarchy. Their goals were instead to institute reforms, to abolish the privileged position of the Germans and the Magyars, and to establish equality among the nations. Of the three principal programs involving the South Slavs, only one envisaged the breakup of the Dual Monarchy. The first, trialism, was closely associated with Franz Ferdinand, the heir to the throne. It called for the formation of a third, Slavic political unit within the empire to balance Austria and Hungary. The second plan supported the creation of an independent Croatian state, separate from Hungary, and also from the empire. The third idea, the creation of a Yugoslavia, was by far the most dangerous for the peace of central Europe. It provided for the unification of the South Slavs of the Habsburg Empire with the Serbs and Montenegrins in a great new state and, inevitably, the destruction of the Dual Monarchy. The erection of a Yugoslav state could, of course, be carried through only with the cooperation of Serbia and Montenegro and their willingness to sacrifice their own national identities to the larger concept.

The dissolution of the Habsburg Empire and the creation of Yugoslavia were finally brought about more by the force of external events than by political action within the monarchy. Particularly important was the increasing antagonism between Vienna and Belgrade. In 1878, in accordance with the Berlin settlement, Austria-Hungary occupied Bosnia-Hercegovina. This action was intended as compensation for the expected Russian domination of Bulgaria. The Austrian move occasioned a violent national reaction in Serbia, for the Serbs felt that the provinces were rightfully theirs. Subsequently, however, Serbia herself fell under the influence of Austria. In 1903, after the assassination of the pro-Habsburg Alexander Obrenović and the assumption of power by Peter Karadjordjević, relations between the two states grew worse. Peter brought his country out of the Austrian orbit and turned to France and Russia for material and moral support. The annexation of Bosnia-Hercegovina by Austria-Hungary in 1908 caused a severe crisis in which all the great powers were involved. Peter also supported a program of national aggrandizement, but the form which this would take was not clear at first.

Serbia had, in fact, several choices in the continuation of her national movement. She could, for example, encourage the Yugoslav concept. This program, however, involved the subordination of the unique individuality of the Serbian state. The greatest obstacle was, perhaps, the religious issue. Orthodoxy in Serbia, as in all Balkan countries, had been the bulwark of nationalism, particularly in times of adversity. Yet in a new Yugoslavia Orthodox Serbs would have to accept as equal—and perhaps even submit to a degree of control from—Catholic Slovenes and Croats. The Serbs thus had to decide whether they were Serbs or Yugoslavs, and most remained convinced that their primary loyalty lay to the Serbian state. Under these conditions, the second idea—that of a greater Serbia—had more appeal. With this policy, Belgrade would seek the incorporation of Bosnia-Hercegovina and parts of Croatia, Slavonia, and Dalmatia from the Habsburg Empire, but the "Piedmont of the Balkans" would retain firm control of the movement. A centralized state—not a federation —would be the result and clear Serbian domination would be established. Nevertheless, the appeal of the Yugoslav idea was recognized and it was employed as a tactical weapon.

It can thus be seen that, although the Yugoslav idea had much appeal, it was not the favored program of the majority of the South Slavs within the empire or in the Kingdom of Serbia. Loyal to their national individuality, the majority of Habsburg Slavs desired autonomy within the empire. The Serbs wished to enlarge their territory, but with no change in their basic state structure or in their own national character.

The story of how this problem became the immediate cause of World War I is a fascinating and complex one. In 1914 Europe went to war after an incident which was instigated by the national resentments and ambitions in Serbia and the Habsburg Empire. Unlike the subjects of the Ottoman Empire, the Slavs of the Habsburg provinces were not the victims of extreme maladministration or continual atrocities. They were, in fact, better governed than the majority of the independent Balkan peoples. When they finally achieved independence, the former Habsburg possessions were to have sometimes less, not more, internal autonomy than they had enjoyed under Habsburg control. As members of the empire, they were also part of a prosperous economic unit and an advanced and cultivated community. Nevertheless, perhaps because of this higher level of cultural development and political awareness, the Habsburg Slavs felt their inferior status within the empire all the more. Conditions within the monarchy were tense, but not desperate. The responsible minority groups did not wish to destroy the state. This condition of national ferment and political controversy might have continued for a long time; the Ottoman Empire, for example, had declined over a period of 250 years. At this time, however, the Balkan peninsula again became involved in the imperial conflicts of the great powers. The situation was further complicated by the appearance of Germany on the Balkan scene.

The unification of Germany brought to the diplomatic stage a new power of tremendous military and economic potential. For the first twenty years after unification, German policy was guided by Otto von Bismarck, who believed that Germany should not pursue a separate policy in the Balkans, but should seek to bring Austria and Russia into agreement on the problems of the area. In 1890 Bismarck left office and the emperor, William II, embarked upon a new course of action. First, he ended the alliance with Russia which Bismarck had considered to be one of the cornerstones of German policy; he renewed only the agreements which Germany had with Austria-Hungary and Italy. He then adopted a most dangerous colonial and naval policy which brought him into conflict with Britain. The simultaneous breaking of the tie with the greatest land power, Russia, and the fostering of antagonism with the foremost sea power, Britain, made Germany more dependent upon her southern ally: Austria-Hungary. Italy, although joined in an alliance with Germany, was not regarded as dependable; France, after her loss of Alsace-Lorraine to Germany in 1870, was always in the opposing camp. At the same time that Germany's dependence upon the Habsburg Empire was increasing, the national agitation within that state was in fact causing a decrease in its military potential. Not only the South Slavs, but the other national minorities as well, were demanding increased political rights. This internal conflict and the possibility that the administration of the empire might be further decentralized made Austria-Hungary a less valuable military ally. Because the existence of the Dual Monarchy was essential for her own security, Germany had a deep interest in the political developments on the Danube. In the 1870s Bismarck had informed Russia that Germany, because of her strategic position, could not allow the severe defeat or destruction of the Danubian monarchy. This principle was even more important in 1914 when that state was, in fact, Germany's only reliable ally.

Although the imperial policies of the European powers were usually directed toward Africa or Asia, the Balkans also became a field for political and economic penetration. Germany and Italy, new national states, joined the older powers in this action. Italy directed her efforts toward securing predominance on the Adriatic and acquiring territory along the Mediterranean. In 1911 she went to war with

THE BALKANS IN 1914

Turkey and took Tripoli and the Greek-inhabited Dodecanese Islands. Germany, through her sponsorship of a Berlin-to-Bagdad railroad, challenged the former supremacy of Britain in the Middle East. She also sought to increase her influence with the Turkish government.

In the nineteenth century, Britain had been the chief supporter of the Ottoman Empire and the main opponent of Balkan nationalism. By 1914 this role, to an extent, had been assumed by the German Empire. The penetration of the new powers, Germany and Italy, into an area where they had previously held the decisive position was naturally opposed by Britain, France, and Russia. Once bitter opponents, these three states had, by the beginning of World War I, joined in a diplomatic alignment: the Triple Entente. The basis of this combination was a strong military alliance between Russia and France and colonial settlements between Britain, France, and Russia. The three powers were also joined by various naval and military arrangements. Opposing this alignment was the Triple Alliance of Germany, Austria-Hungary, and Italy, which had been formed by Bismarck and subsequently renewed at regular intervals.

On the eve of World War I, the three empires—Russia, Austria-Hungary, and Turkey—were clearly in a state of decline. After the Revolution of 1905, Russia became, in theory, a constitutional monarchy; the reform, however, failed to calm internal agitation. Russia remained deeply involved in Balkan affairs; the annexation of Bosnia-Hercegovina by Austria-Hungary in 1908 had damaged Russian prestige. Because of internal difficulties and diplomatic setbacks, the Russian government could not afford another humiliation in the Balkans.

The political unrest evident in Russia and the Habsburg Empire was also reflected in the Balkan states. The Macedonian problem had become infinitely complicated by the activities of terrorist organizations, the most notorious of which was the Internal Macedonian Revolutionary Committee (IMRO), whose activities continued into the postwar period. Similar societies existed among the Serbs. The most important of these was called "Union or Death," better known as "The Black Hand." This group, formed in 1911 with the aim of bringing about the union of all the Serbs, operated within Serbia, often in defiance of the government itself. Officials of the Serbian state and army were among its members and the government was not able to control its operations.

Sarajevo

In the summer of 1914, Franz Ferdinand, the heir to the Habsburg throne, made an official visit to Sarajevo, the capital of Bosnia-Hercegovina. He arrived on June 28th, the anniversary of the battle of Kosovo, the Serbian national holiday. There he was assassinated by a young Bosnian student, Gavrilo Princip. Princip's weapon had been illegally obtained from a Serbian state arsenal and he had been assisted across the frontier by Serbian officials who were members of the Black Hand. The Austrian reaction was remarkably slow. For three weeks an investigation was conducted. Finally, on July 23rd, the Habsburg government delivered an ultimatum with a forty-eight-hour time limit. When Serbia's reply proved unsatisfactory, Austria-Hungary declared war.

The subsequent involvement of the other European great powers need not concern us in detail. Each was drawn in by its obligations to its allies, by military necessity, and by considerations of national honor and prestige. The Triple Entente—Russia, France, and Britain—joined with Serbia against Germany and Austria-Hungary. Italy, the third member of the Triple Alliance, chose to remain neutral for the time being.

FIVE

WORLD WAR I AND

THE PEACE SETTLEMENTS

World War I, a major disaster for Europe as a whole, brought about the completion of the national unification of the Balkan states and the simultaneous downfall of the three great empires —the Habsburg, the Ottoman, and the Russian—which had previously played a predominant role in Balkan history. Few of those who witnessed the commencement of the war in 1914 expected such a revolutionary outcome. For a hundred years Europe had enjoyed relative peace. The conflicts between the nations had been limited in extent and duration or fought on colonial battlefields. No nation in 1914 realized what lay ahead or that the world which was to emerge from the war would be quite different from that which it had previously known.

The Balkan States in the War

The major campaigns of the war were waged in northern France and in Russia. The Balkan area, although involved, remained a secondary field of military activity. At first Serbia was the only belligerent among the Balkan states. The other nations waited and weighed the situation. None could afford to support the losing side; each also wanted the assurance of future rewards in return for possible involvement in the conflict.

The first decision to intervene was made by the Ottoman Empire, which joined the Central Powers. The entrance of Turkey into the conflict meant that the Straits were closed to Allied shipping and that therefore the major sea lane between Russia and her western partners was cut.

The second Balkan state to enter the war was Bulgaria. In 1914 the outnumbered Serbian armies put up a brave resistance to Austria, which was faced with the problem of meeting a Russian invasion at the same time. The Central Powers, therefore, needed Bulgarian assistance against Serbia. Bulgaria was thus in a good position to bargain with both sides. The Allies offered parts of Thrace and Macedonia, but the Central Powers bid higher and offered Bulgaria more Serbian territory. Moreover, the pro-German King Ferdinand was convinced that the Central Powers would win the war. In October 1915 Bulgaria declared war and the Serbian army was doomed. Driven across the Montenegrin and Albanian mountains in winter, the Serbian forces suffered tremendous losses. The survivors were evacuated to Corfu.

Rumania was the next state to join the conflict. The Central Powers offered her Bessarabia, but the Allies promised Transylvania. In this situation, the second choice was obviously the better one. In August 1916—in return for the assurance that she would receive Transylvania, Bukovina, and other territories belonging to Hungary— Rumania went to war. Not only did she back the eventual winner, but another event came to her aid. In 1917 the Russian armies collapsed and in the next year Russia concluded the Treaty of Brest-Litovsk with the Central Powers. In the turmoil which resulted in Russia from the lost war and the Bolshevik Revolution, Rumanian troops were able to enter Bessarabia. At the peace conference, therefore, Rumania had a great advantage: she was already in possession of one of her unredeemed territories and she had the promise of others.

Thus three Balkan states—Turkey, Bulgaria, and Rumania—entered the war on the assurance of future rewards and after careful calculation. The fourth Balkan power, Greece, was faced with a more difficult decision because of the contrary opinions of the king, Constantine, who was the brother-in-law of the German emperor, and his chief minister, Venizelos, who favored the Allies. The country was thus divided into two camps on the issue of participation in the war. In 1915 Venizelos allowed the Allies to land troops in Thessaloniki, where they established a huge encampment of 150,000 officers and men. The king nevertheless managed to keep the country officially neutral. In October 1916, in a full break with the king, Venizelos established a revolutionary government in Thessaloniki which was immediately recognized by the Allies. An Allied fleet was sent to Piraeus and the king was informed that Athens would be shelled if he did not abdicate. With Constantine removed, Greece entered the war in July 1917.

By the summer of 1918 it was clear that the German armies in France were losing their power of attack. In September the Allied forces in Thessaloniki, until then mostly inactive, launched their great offensive. By the end of the month, Bulgaria had surrendered and Constantinople was exposed to attack from the north. Because he had also suffered defeats in other parts of his lands, the sultan sued for peace. The crumbling of the Balkan flank of the Central Powers had a disastrous effect on the Habsburg Empire: it literally broke apart into its ethnic components, each of which now aimed at gaining complete political independence. Germany surrendered in November. Russia, thrown into chaos by war and revolution, was no longer in a position to play a role in European diplomacy. With the elimination of these governments, the peace treaties were drawn up by the four victorious states: France, Britain, Italy (which had joined the Allies in 1915), and the United States, a new power in the European balance.

The Peace Settlements

The significance of the entrance of the United States into the war was not only the role which its wealth and military strength played in the achievement of final victory, but also the influence which President Wilson's ideas on foreign policy were to have on the postwar settlements. Believing that a lasting peace could be obtained only through the application of just principles in international relations, Wilson supported the idea of self-determination in the drawing of national boundaries. He was opposed by those who stood to gain through the secret treaties which had been made during the war and by those who wished to use the peace settlement to guarantee their future predominance. Many also quite justly questioned the practicality and applicability of some of Wilson's concepts. In the Balkans the conflict on this question centered on the issue of the boundaries of a Yugoslav state and Albania.

YUGOSLAVIA. Although in the prewar period the desire to create a Yugoslav state had not commanded the support of the majority of the South Slavs in the Habsburg Empire, the events of the war led to a change of opinion, particularly among the Croats. As the war progressed, the loyalty of the Slavic citizens to the monarchy gradually weakened. Despite the fact that most Croats fought loyally for the Habsburg Empire, particularly against the Italians, the influence of those who sought a separation from Vienna and Budapest grew. In 1917, in the Declaration of Corfu, Nikola Pašić, the head of the Serbian government-in-exile, and Ante Trumbić, who represented a committee of the leading South Slav politicians from the empire (but who were now abroad) agreed upon the creation of a state which would include Serbs, Croats, and Slovenes. The Karadjordjević dynasty was to rule, but no decision was taken on whether the state was to have a federal or centralized form of government. The basis was nevertheless laid for the formation of a Yugoslav state. Moreover, the Croats and the Slovenes, because of the attitude of the other nationalities in the empire, no longer had the alternative of seeking an autonomous status within the Dual Monarchy. By the end of the war it was clear that the Habsburg Empire could not be held together.

The drawing of the boundaries for the new kingdom—which at first was not called Yugoslavia, but the Kingdom of the Serbs, Croats, and Slovenes—caused a major conflict with Italy at the Versailles Peace Conference. Italy, despite its alliance with the Central Powers, had entered the war in 1915 on the Allied side on the basis of the Treaty of London. This agreement promised Italy wide territorial gains in Yugoslav lands, including Dalmatia and the Adriatic islands. At the conference, Wilson opposed fulfilling the treaty stipulations because they violated the principle of self-determination. Although Italy did not receive the major portion of her claims, she did obtain Istria, the port of Fiume (Rijeka), Zara (Zadar), and Trieste. The annexation of Istria, with its predominantly Croat and Slovene population, embittered the postwar relations of Italy and Yugoslavia.

The Yugoslav state created at Versailles was about three times the size of prewar Serbia. To the former Serbian kingdom were added the Slovenian provinces of Carinthia and Carniola, and Croatian Dalmatia (former Austrian territories); Croatia, Slavonia, and the Vojvodina (former Hungarian possessions); and Bosnia-Hercegovina (which had been administered jointly by Austria and Hungary). In 1918 Montenegro voted for union with the new nation. The creation of this large and potentially powerful state was the major transformation which occurred in the Balkans as the result of the war.

RUMANIA. Rumania was the next beneficiary of the Allied victory. As has been mentioned, Rumania had occupied Bessarabia during the war. A similar course of action was followed in Transylvania. Rumanian possession of this province was confirmed at the Versailles Peace Conference. The simultaneous destruction of the military power of her two neighbors, Russia and Austria-Hungary, was, of course, also an immense gain. After the war, Rumania, doubled in size, became the largest of the Balkan states.

GREECE. Despite the fact that she was in the camp of the victors, Greece received very little for her participation in the war. Like the Yugoslavs, the Greeks found many of their claims opposed by the Italians. Although Greece received from Bulgaria a section of Thrace, which cut the northern state from the Aegean Sea, Italy kept the Dodecanese Islands and Britain retained Cyprus. Greek attempts to gain a larger share of the postwar spoils resulted in a national disaster.

As her share in the division of the Asiatic possessions of the Ottoman Empire, Greece was allowed to occupy the city of Smyrna (Izmir) and the surrounding territory, which had many Greek inhabitants. The region was to be administered by Greece for five years, at the end of which a plebiscite was to determine the final disposition of the area. Unfortunately, Venizelos, not content with Greece's share, came to the opinion that it would be possible to form a great Greek province in Asia Minor. Venizelos was forced out of office when King Constantine returned in 1920, but the adventure in Anatolia was not abandoned. In March 1921 Greek troops started out from Smyrna to march into the heart of the Turkish territory. The undertaking was doomed from the start. Under the leadership of Mustafa Kemal, the defeated Turkey had undergone a great national revival. The new Turkish government now had the diplomatic support of France, Italy, and Soviet Russia, who resented the fact that Britain had taken the lion's share of the spoils of war in the former Ottoman territories.

In their march into Anatolia the Greek troops, with no foreign assistance, soon ran into difficulties. They advanced so rapidly at first that they soon outdistanced their lines of supply. Deep within Turkey, they were defeated and forced back to the sea. The Turks, again in Smyrna, destroyed the Greek city. At this time—and later, in a series of population transfers—the Greek inhabitants of the area were forced to move to Greece. As a result of the reckless and ill-planned campaign, Greece was compelled to receive almost 1.3 million Greek refugees. Her total population was at the time only about 4.5 million. The Turks also won back a part of Thrace and two islands. Greece thus not only lost territory, but she was also forced to provide for a destitute and suffering refugee population that was suddenly thrust upon her. The disaster forced Constantine to abdicate in 1922 in favor of his son, George II.

ALBANIA. Despite the fact that the troops of both the Central Powers and the Allies had marched through the country, Albania survived the war remarkably well. With the hostilities over, however, Greece, Yugoslavia, and Italy immediately pressed their claims on Albanian territory. Had they been successful, the state established in 1912 would have been partitioned and destroyed. Once again Woodrow Wilson took a strong stand in favor of the principle of self-determination. Athough Albania remained intact, the threat from her neighbors continued.

BULGARIA. As the one nation in the Balkans which had supported the losing side, Bulgaria was bound to suffer for her mistake. In a frankly vindictive peace settlement that was not based on the principle of self-determination—a concept which the victorious Balkan states had enthusiastically supported when their own claims were in question—Bulgaria lost western Thrace and four strategic areas along the Yugoslav frontier. In addition, an indemnity of $450 million was levied upon her, a sum beyond her capacity to pay. This harsh peace embittered relations among the Balkan countries and precluded any real possibility of cooperation with Bulgaria after the war.

The end of World War I thus marked the final stage in the establishment of the modern Balkan states. Except for Rumania's loss of Bessarabia to the Soviet Union, Yugoslavia's acquisition of Istria, Fiume, Zara, and several minor islands, Bulgaria's securing of southern Dobrudja, and Italy's cession of the Dodecanese islands to Greece, World War II brought no further major changes in the Balkan boundaries. Two states—Yugoslavia and Rumania—benefited most from the partition of the former possessions of the Ottoman

Empire and the Habsburg Empire. Not only were their territories now extensive, but they were also well enough endowed economically to give the hope for a relatively prosperous future. On the other end of the scale, Bulgaria and Albania suffered most in the division of the former Ottoman lands. After losing two wars in succession, Bulgaria was excluded from a real share in the partition of Turkish Thrace and Macedonia. Albania saw one third of her population remain under Serbian control and another section under Greek rule. Of the Balkan states, Greece occupied a middle position. Although she received a share in the division of Thrace and Macedonia, the establishment of national states in the Balkans actually marked a strong contraction of Greek influence in the Balkans and the Near East. The greatest disaster was the expulsion of the Greek population from Asia Minor. A large number of these people were subsequently settled in Greek Macedonia, which—with the departure of the Bulgarian and Turkish inhabitants through population exchanges—now acquired a clearly Greek character. Equally disadvantageous to Greek influence and prestige was the expulsion of the Greeks from Bulgaria and Yugoslavia. The Greeks had always played an important role in the commercial life of these states, but the pressure of national hatred now led them to resettle in Greece. These people, who in the eighteenth century had been the most prosperous and favored of the Christians in the Ottoman Empire, and who had settled and carried on trade throughout the Mediterranean and Black Sea area, were now forced back upon a homeland that could ill afford to receive them.

Thus a century of national liberation in the Balkans ended with the freeing of the subject peoples from Ottoman and Habsburg control. New problems and further tension between the nations were, however, also created. Although the Albanians, the Bulgarians, and the Greeks now had their own national states, they had paid an enormous price for freedom and they were not satisfied either with their boundaries or with their relative position in the area. Yugoslavia and Rumania, the favored nations, were to find in the next twenty years that the unification of peoples with different historical traditions and cultures could present problems so grave as to endanger the safety of the state.

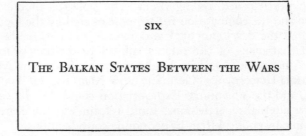

SIX

THE BALKAN STATES BETWEEN THE WARS

In the nineteenth century, the main efforts of each Balkan nation had been devoted to the national question; until this issue was settled it was almost impossible to concentrate on any other. With the achievement of national liberation and unification after World War I, it could be expected that the Balkan governments would turn their attention toward the development of the internal resources of their countries and the improvement of their administrations. The relatively brief period between the two great wars of the twentieth century was, however, as perilous and as difficult a time for the Balkan states as it was for the great powers. During these twenty years the Balkan nations faced the same world economic crises that shattered far more prosperous countries. Political developments in the Balkans therefore followed the general pattern of central Europe and witnessed the same evolution from a parliamentary system to a military dictatorship.

The Peasant Problem

Concentration on their internal improvement and development was certainly the first need of all of the Balkan nations after the end of World War I. In 1923 the Balkan states had the following populations: Rumania: 17.5 million; Yugoslavia: 12 million; Greece: 5.5 million; Albania: 800,000. Of this number the peasantry constituted 78 per cent of the population in Rumania, 75 per cent in Yugoslavia, 80 per cent in Bulgaria and 60 per cent in Greece. It was in this, the larger section of the population, that conditions not only failed to improve, but actually declined in the years before 1939.

After the war, internal political pressures forced all of the states to undertake land reform. The peasants in each country were convinced that conditions would automatically be improved if only the large holdings were divided among them. The political circumstances of the time and the competition for support offered by the Communists accelerated the development. Land reform was also made easier by the fact that many of the estates subject to division were held by "enemy" nationals. Moslem landowners dominated in Macedonia and Bosnia-Hercegovina; Germans and Magyars, in Transylvania, Croatia, and the Vojvodina. Expropriation could thus be carried out with few internal repercussions. Land reform was therefore brought about more by political than by economic considerations.

Unfortunately, the consequences of the action were not realized at the time. The redistribution of the land, instead of improving the lot of the peasant, often contributed to depressing rural conditions. The Balkan population rose sharply after World War I. Life was more secure and improvements in medicine and hygiene had caused a drop in the death rate. In the western countries the enormous population growths could be absorbed by expanding economies and growing industrial plants. In the Balkans these outlets were not available; the result was a heavy rural overpopulation. The prevailing customs on the distribution of property did not help to ease the situation. Because the land at the death of the owner was divided among his sons, extreme fragmentation of holdings occurred. Moreover, to secure an equal distribution of good and bad land, each heir might receive a number of scattered plots. Much space was wasted in footpaths between and around minute pieces. The average holdings in many places were so small that they required only a fraction of the working time of their owners. Thus too many people were available for too little work. As one authority concludes: "the majority of the people in the Balkan village were not needed."[1]

The division of the land into small holdings also prevented economic and rational use of the land. The greatest agricultural production usually comes from large units which are worked by scientific methods and machines rather than by hand tools and animals. The small plots were not suitable for modern agricultural techniques, and

[1] L. S. Stavrianos, *The Balkans Since 1453* (New York: Holt, Rinehart & Winston, Inc., 1958), p. 595.

the peasants were too poor to afford even the basic tools and chemicals required to increase the production on their land. Moreover, the replacement of human labor by machinery, necessary for the real improvement of agricultural conditions, would only have contributed to the problem of rural overpopulation. Unless the surplus peasant population could emigrate or move to the city, modern techniques would only aggravate the social ills. Thus the Balkan states were caught in a vicious circle of rising population figures, increasing fragmentation of land-holdings, and a constantly falling standard of living.

The agricultural depression was reflected in the life and health of the people. The rates for tuberculosis, rickets, and infant mortality—all closely associated with malnutrition—were the highest in Europe. The extremely primitive living conditions in the villages and the limited, meager diet of the peasants mirrored their miserable economic plight. The world depression of the 1930s caused a further deterioration in the situation. At that time the demand for agricultural products dropped and the difference between farm prices and those of manufactured goods widened.

The political organization of the Balkan states also operated to the disadvantage of the Balkan peasant. Although they constituted the vast majority of the population in the Balkan countries, the peasants and the far more limited number of industrial laborers were usually effectively excluded from political power. Immediately after the war, agrarian parties appeared in Bulgaria, Croatia, and Rumania, and for a short time they were able to control or influence the government. Soon, however, they lost either their influence or their peasant character. Political power thus remained in the hands of those who had held it previously—the comparatively small governing class, which held its superior position through wealth, education, and its control of the police and army. Political life was still carried on under constitutional forms. Most states continued to hold elections until the late 1930s. Political parties were, however, built around single individuals or groups. Politics became the question of the struggle between individuals who represented the same social and economic group, not a debate over issues. The fraudulent practices that underlay the electoral procedures of the nineteenth century were carried over into the twentieth.

This inequality of power, privilege, and wealth resulted in a schism in each country. City life was Westernized. French customs and civilization were particularly admired. Life in the countryside, in contrast, remained relatively unchanged and continued to reflect the unique aspects of each national culture. The growing difference between the city and the countryside led to the creation of two separate societies within each state. Those in power enjoyed the advantages of Western life; the rest lived in conditions closely resembling those under which they had suffered for centuries past.

Attempts at Industrialization

At the end of the nineteenth century, attempts had been made to build up Balkan industry. It was obvious that the wealthiest and most powerful states of Europe were those with the greatest industrial plants. The Balkan governments wished to follow in the modern path. Industrialization was also seen as a means of alleviating rural overpopulation. From the beginning, however, Balkan industrialization encountered grave obstacles. First, because local funds were not available, foreign loans and foreign investors had to be relied upon and the cost of these was high. Also, the foreign concerns developed those fields which would yield them a large, immediate profit and, quite naturally, they showed little concern for the welfare of the country as a whole. Another consideration which hampered Balkan economic growth was the deep involvement of the government and of government officials in the development of the industry and resources of the countries. Here again corruption was widespread. Officials sold concessions to industrial concerns and accepted bribes and favors.

The process of industrialization also added to the burden upon the peasantry. Prohibitively high tariffs were placed on those foreign goods which competed with native industry. The peasant thus often found himself paying inflated prices for inferior products. Tariffs were also placed on items such as fertilizers and farm machinery, which were needed on the land. By the beginning of World War II the industrial development of the Balkan states had not reached the level that would help to relieve the problem of rural overpopulation. The peasant had therefore derived very little benefit from the development for which he had paid so high a price.

Political Developments

Between the wars the Balkan governments were neither in theory nor in practice social welfare states. Social measures were usually not

THE BALKANS BETWEEN THE WORLD WARS

regarded as part of normal governmental activity. Few efforts were made to improve life in the country at large. Instead, the resources of the nation were devoted to the attempt to duplicate in the major cities the general circumstances of life in the wealthy nations and to create a first-class army. The provision and equipment of a modern military establishment was a great burden on the finances of all the Balkan states and, in fact, precluded adequate domestic development. The problems of immediate concern to the population, particularly in the fields of communication and health, were neglected. General education was badly provided for. In 1938 the rate of illiteracy varied from 25 per cent in Greece to 85 per cent in Albania. The quality of instruction in the schools was not high; those who could afford it sent their children abroad to study. Those who remained at home received a nationalistic view of their own past which emphasized their points of superiority and their neighbors' deficiencies.

Beset by grave social and economic problems, each Balkan state moved gradually toward an outright military dictatorship. It must be repeated that this twenty-year period between the wars was not a normal time. Every European government was faced with difficulties very similar to those in the Balkans. The Balkan governments were faced by almost permanent conditions of crisis. All were at war from 1912 to 1918. Greece fought until 1923. No sooner had the damage from the war been repaired than the entire world felt the effects of the Great Depression. Thereafter the rise of aggressive military dictatorships in Germany and Italy made necessary continued military preparation by the Balkan governments. The political evolution of the Balkans must therefore always be viewed against that of the rest of Europe. Few governments can look back to the 1930s with any great feeling of satisfaction.

BULGARIA. Having lost the war, Bulgaria alone among the Balkan states had no problems in connection with the administration of new territories. The military defeat forced King Ferdinand to abdicate in favor of his son, Boris III. Thereafter the political evolution of the country duplicated that of the other Balkan states. In 1919 Alexander Stamboliski, the peasant party leader, became premier after an election in which the Agrarian and Communist parties together received 70 per cent of the vote. During his four years in office, Stamboliski attempted to introduce many reform measures. After six years of war and two defeats, the Bulgarians were weary of conflict and ready for change. Although Bulgaria was already the most equalitarian of the Balkan nations in regard to land holding, a redistribution of state lands and large farms was undertaken. Reforms were also introduced in the tax system, the administration of justice, and education. In the international field, the premier called for a policy of friendship with Bulgaria's neighbors, particularly Yugoslavia, and supported the idea of a South Slav federation or a Balkan Union. He also favored the formation of a Green International, a union of the peasant parties of Europe which would stand against the Red International of the Communists and the White International of the reaction.

Stamboliski's measures, and the methods he used to put them through, stirred up a great deal of opposition in both the Right and the Left. Moreover, many of his followers in the peasant party were not experienced in government; like their predecessors, they proved corruptible and high-handed. Particularly unpopular was the new attitude toward Yugoslavia. For years the conflict over Macedonia had dominated Bulgarian foreign policy. The fact that Bulgaria had not gained what she regarded as her national territory did not make her citizens more peacefully inclined. Also, the country was flooded with refugees from Yugoslav- and Greek-controlled Macedonian territories. These people, uprooted from their own lands, found it hard to find a place in Bulgaria. More difficult to handle was the problem of IMRO. This organization, like the prewar Black Hand in Serbia, proved too strong for the regular government to control. Its members joined with other opposition elements in 1923 in a military *coup* which resulted in the assassination of Stamboliski. Although the Communists did not at first come to the aid of the Agrarian party, they soon staged another uprising which was put down with great force. Stamboliski was the only peasant leader in the interwar years who was in a position to demonstrate what an agrarian regime could do. When he failed, the record of his administration and his personal fate tended to discredit peasant leaders in the other Balkan states. The peasant parties never recovered from this setback.

The new premier, Alexander Tsankov, also proved unable to control the country. In southwestern Bulgaria IMRO formed a state within a state and terrorized the country. In 1934 another military *coup* was organized under the leadership of Colonel Damian Velchev. His victory led to an improvement of the internal conditions. Although his Military League dissolved the political parties, it was also able to break the power of IMRO. This organization never again dominated the political life of the state. In 1935 King Boris was able to reassert the power of the throne and to reduce that of the military. He established a royal dictatorship which lasted until his death in 1943. He maintained the prohibition on political parties, and kept a firm hold on the country through the police and the army. In 1938 national elections were held, but the candidates were permitted to run only as individuals, not as members of parties. Even with this measure, a third of the assembly was in opposition to the regime. Because the assembly had only consultative powers, it could do little to limit the authority of the king. Thus Bulgaria, which had begun the postwar period with the most promising of the Balkan peasant parties in control, ended with a strong military dictatorship under the king.

RUMANIA. Events in neighboring Rumania followed a similar course. Rumania, with her annexation of Bessarabia and Transylvania, emerged from the war with the richest gains of the Balkan nations. Although the amalgamation of these lands gave rise to severe problems, these issues did not tear apart the state as they did in Yugoslavia. In the immediate postwar years, a series of land reforms was introduced by the predominant Liberal party. These were designed to limit the power of the Conservative party, which represented the owners of the large estates. Much of the land to be divided belonged to other than Rumanian owners. The division of Hungarian property in Transylvania was not an unpopular measure. With a single short break, the Liberal party, under the leadership of Ion Bratianu, remained in power from 1922 to 1927. This long tenure in office was possible because the king favored the party and the government used police control. The period of Liberal party power was also a time of further attempts at industrialization.

The problem of the government of Transylvania became an issue after the promulgation of the constitution of 1923, which made Rumania a centralized state. Officials from Bucharest were sent to administer Transylvanian affairs. This imposition of central control was resented in the province, which had enjoyed a larger measure of self-government under Hungarian rule. In 1926 a new party was formed in protest. The National Peasant party, as it was known, was composed of those who wished more local rights in Transylvania and of former members of the prewar peasant party.

In 1927 King Ferdinand died. His son, Carol, was excluded from the succession because of his liaison with Magda Lupescu, whom the prince would not leave. Under the circumstances, a regency was formed to rule in the name of Carol's son, Michael. In 1928 elections were held; these, in contrast to the majority of elections held in the country, were considered honest. The National Peasant party, under the leadership of Julius Maniu, gained over 330 representatives in the national assembly; the Liberals received thirteen. The peasant party which now came to power in Rumania had much in common with that of Stamboliski in Bulgaria. Maniu's party held power but a short time. In 1930 Carol returned to Rumania from abroad and sought to re-establish his power. Maniu agreed, but on the condition that Carol leave Magda Lupescu. When the king later resumed the relationship, the Peasant party leader resigned. Maniu's period in government had not been a great success. It coincided with the commencement of the Great Depression, which greatly affected Rumanian grain exports. There was also too little time for the enactment of reforms. As in Bulgaria, the peasant representatives had often been guilty of the same scandals that had characterized the earlier regimes.

After his return, Carol became the chief political figure in the country. The parliamentary institutions remained, but the king was able to control the politicians and the parties. The 1930s brought the rise of the only truly Fascist party in the Balkans: the Iron Guard. The organization was, however, opposed by the king, who correctly saw it as a challenge to his power. In 1938 a new constitution was drawn up which, like that of Bulgaria, abolished all political parties and gave the king absolute control. Carol then turned upon the Iron Guard; its leader was shot "while trying to escape" and the organization was dissolved. Like Bulgaria, Rumania was now under a royal dictatorship. Carol kept his power through the support of the army and the conservative elements and through the use of clever political tactics.

GREECE. Political conditions in Greece in the postwar period differed from those in Bulgaria and Rumania. In Greece, for instance, peasant parties were absent from the political scene. In addition, the position of the king was always weaker in Greece than in the other Balkan states. In fact, the chief political issue between the wars concerned the maintenance or abolition of the monarchy. The role of the king in Greece had been a difficult one since the establishment of the Greek state in 1832. He was usually made the scapegoat for any failure in foreign policy. Othon's fate demonstrated this circumstance; Constantine I and George II were also forced to abdicate when the government met defeat abroad. Because the king lacked real popular support, he was always dependent on the backing of the army. As long as he retained control of the military, he kept his throne. When the army fell under the influence of elements hostile to the monarchy, the king went into exile.

Postwar Greece also had to face economic problems which were more severe than those of any Balkan state except Albania. With only a quarter of her land area suitable for agriculture, Greece had to import 50 per cent of her food. This situation was made worse when the 1.3 million refugees from the debacle in Asia Minor poured into the country. Unfortunately, no Greek government in the interwar period made a real effort to meet the basic economic problems of Greece. Instead, Greek political life revolved around the issue of the monarchy and the continuation of old quarrels with neighboring states.

After the failure of the campaign in Turkey, the king was forced to abdicate and the army fell under republican control. The first period of the republic, which lasted from 1924 to 1936, was marked by a series of crises in foreign affairs. In 1923 the Italian members of a border commission were murdered on Greek soil. In retaliation Italy occupied the island of Corfu until an indemnity was paid. In 1925 a border incident took place and Greek troops entered Bulgaria. In this case, both countries were finally compelled by the League of Nations to pay fines. Next, conflict with Yugoslavia arose over the question of a free port at Thessaloniki. Finally, Greek and Turkish relations, even after the agreements on the exchange of populations, remained uneasy. The chief issues between them were the position of the Patriarch and the Greek population in Istanbul.

In 1928 Venizelos was returned to office, and he held power until 1933. During this period he was faced with the great problems caused by the world depression, the effects of which were more serious in Greece than in any other Balkan country. The chief Greek exports—tobacco, olives, olive oil, currants, and wine—were luxury items; the demand for these fell sharply. Tourism, another source of income, was similarly affected. At the same time, incidents involving British rule occurred on the island of Cyprus. Unable to find a satisfactory solution to these problems, Venizelos lost popularity and was finally forced to resign. In 1935 a military *coup* brought about the fall of the republic and the return of George II. Thereafter the army firmly supported the monarchy.

Unlike Carol in Rumania or Boris in Bulgaria, George II did not assume a dominant political role. In 1936 he allowed General Metaxas, the head of a small Rightist group, to form a government. The general quickly asserted his personal power, dissolved parliament, and abolished the constitution. In his relations with Metaxas, George II played a role similar to that of the king of Italy under Mussolini. The general, never a popular figure in the country as a whole, held power with the support of the king, the police, and the army until his death in 1941. Thus Greece joined the ranks of the Balkan dictatorships.

ALBANIA. The smallest of the Balkan states, Albania, followed in the political path of her larger neighbors. By far the most backward state in the Balkans, Albania had no good educational system and no satisfactory internal communications. The best lands were in the large estates owned by Moslem landlords. The rivalry between the Ghegs and the Tosks made it difficult to establish a stable government. The period 1920-24 was one of internal reorganization. Two important leaders emerged: the first, Bishop Fan S. Noli, had an American background and favored a more democratic organization; the second, Ahmed Zog, supported the interests of the Moslem landowners. In 1924, amidst great political turmoil, Zog was forced to flee into Yugoslavia. From there, with the aid of Yugoslav forces, he launched a successful invasion of his own country. In 1925 Albania was declared a republic and Zog was elected president for a term of seven years.

The Albanian republic lasted from 1925 to 1928. Under the constitution of 1925, the president had the real power in the state. Zog gave his close followers the principal offices in the government. The greatest weakness of the country was its immense poverty. Assistance to improve internal conditions was first sought from the League of Nations. When no aid could be obtained from this source, Albania had no alternative but to turn to Italy, which used the opportunity to gain control over the country. Italy established the national bank of Albania, which issued money, gave loans, and supervised the economic life of the country. In 1926 the Tirana Pact was concluded; in 1927 a defensive military alliance was effected. These agreements made Albania a protectorate of Italy.

Zog did not remain content with the position of president. In 1928 he was crowned king and changed the constitution. After 1931 he made a strong attempt to limit Italian influence. Because Italy at the time was engaged in war in Ethiopia and was involved in the Spanish Civil War, Zog did have some success. In March 1939, however, Hitler marched into Prague and brought about the dismemberment of Czechoslovakia. Mussolini was not altogether pleased with the gain in prestige and power which this act had given his German ally. To re-establish his own position, the Italian dictator turned on Albania and, in April 1939, issued an ultimatum demanding that Albania become an open protectorate of Italy. When Zog rejected the terms, the Italian armies invaded this country. Albania was thereafter annexed to Italy and Victor Emmanuel was declared king. Thus, on the eve of World War II, Albania lost her independence.

YUGOSLAVIA. The most interesting developments in the internal affairs of the Balkan states in the interwar period occurred in Yugoslavia. In the nineteenth century, as has been shown, the Balkan nations, like the rest of Europe, put their faith in the national principle. All the people in the Balkans had made bitter sacrifices to achieve independence. The chief difficulty faced by the Balkan governments in the late nineteenth and twentieth centuries was not that of defeating the weak Ottoman Empire, but that of drawing boundaries between the nations. This issue became most apparent in the struggle over Macedonia. The great difficulty in defining the term *nationality* and the practical application of the principle of self-determination, even when it was accepted, was also shown in the internal developments in Yugoslavia almost immediately after its establishment in 1919.

The Kingdom of the Serbs, Croats, and Slovenes (which will be referred to as *Yugoslavia* hereafter for the sake of clarity) was formed from the historic lands of Serbia and Montenegro, and from the former Habsburg regions of Bosnia-Hercegovina, Slovenia, Dalmatia, Croatia, Slavonia, and the Vojvodina, each of which had its own unique character and traditions. These areas had three religions. The Moslems were strong, although not dominant, in Bosnia-Hercegovina; Catholicism was predominant in most of the former Habsburg lands; Orthodoxy was the religion of Serbia, Macedonia, and Montenegro. Yugoslavia also contained three general levels of political and cultural development. The former Habsburg possessions had been comparatively well administered and had been part of an ad-

vanced culture. Serbia and Montenegro, which had been independent, had a long and vigorous national tradition. Macedonia, which
had only recently been freed from Ottoman control, had the lowest
level of development. Bosnia-Hercegovina was somewhat more advanced than Macedonia, because of forty years of Austro-Hungarian
occupation. All these were now joined together in one state.

Although Yugoslavism had been a definite political force before
the war, it had been mainly an intellectual and literary concept. As
an idea it certainly never won the broad popular support enjoyed by
the national movements in Greece, Bulgaria, Serbia, or Montenegro
at the time of their fight for liberation from foreign rule. After World
War I the Croats and Slovenes had no choice but to join the new
state. The Habsburg Empire could not be resurrected and the two
nations were too weak to form independent states of their own. The
Serbs supported the union because of the obvious difference in power
between the old land-locked Serbia and the new Yugoslavia in which
they were predominant. Although it was to the advantage of all the
groups to join in a larger political unit, this association did not automatically bring about the creation of a Yugoslav nationality and a
Yugoslav mentality—nor did it lead the various peoples to put the
needs of the new state before those of their own region. Throughout
the interwar period most of the citizens of Yugoslavia thought of
themselves first as Serbs, Croats, Slovenes, or Macedonians, a condition which still prevails. The sharp division within the country was
shown in the early quarrels over the organization of the government.

Because the difference in their historical experience was so great, it
was perhaps inevitable that the Serbs and the Croats should disagree
on political matters. Since the Middle Ages the Croats had been
accustomed to living in a federal relationship with another nation.
They had not objected to the principle of association with Vienna
and Budapest, but to the fact that the agreements were constantly
broken. They therefore wished to continue this type of relationship
with Serbia and to have control over their own internal administration. The Serbs, in contrast, had no experience with this type of
government. Their own state was strongly centralized and their long
military history had made them a tightly knit national unit. Proud of
their power and leadership in the past, the Serbs saw Yugoslavia
more as a "Greater Serbia" in which Belgrade would rule the other
sections through a centralized administration and control of the army
and foreign affairs.

The difference in viewpoint between the Serbs and the Croats was reflected in the composition and the programs of the two major political parties. In Serbia, the Radical party of Nikola Pašić, which had held power from 1903 to 1914, remained in control. After the war it abandoned its reform program and emphasized the idea of a Greater Serbia. In Croatia, the Croatian Peasant party of Stjepan Radić won the greatest support. This party was the single major group among the Habsburg South Slavs that had not wished for union with Serbia. It led the postwar fight against Serbian centralism, but with very little success. The first trial of strength came over the question of the constitution. Pašić, by very sharp political tactics and cooperation with the Moslems of Bosnia-Hercegovina, was able to obtain the form he wanted. The constitution of 1921, like the Serbian constitution of 1903, provided for a highly centralized state, with a unicameral legislature. The king was given much power and the government had the authority to restrict civil rights.

Thereafter Yugoslavia was governed from Belgrade. Serbia dominated internal affairs, foreign policy, and the army. Most of the ambassadors and almost all the generals were Serbs. The administration was inefficient and corrupt. In 1926 Pašić died and in 1928 Radić was shot, in the assembly, by a Montenegrin member of the Radical party. With the death of these two leaders, the situation further deteriorated.

In this moment of crisis King Alexander took over the government. The new leader of the Croatian Peasant party, Vladko Maček, now demanded a reorganization of the state into federal units. Instead, Alexander abolished the constitution, dissolved the assembly, and set up a royal dictatorship. The constitution of 1931 delivered all the power of the state into his hands. Refusing to yield to separatist demands, Alexander now proceeded to centralize the government further. In 1929 a royal decree changed the name of the country to the "Kingdom of Yugoslavia." The king then divided the state into nine provinces, none of which corresponded to the historic divisions. These units were then named after rivers or other distinguishing geographic features. Alexander's dictatorship marked a period of repression, not only of Croatian nationalism, but also of the parties of the Left. In 1934, Alexander was assassinated by Croatian terrorists, who had Italian and Hungarian backing. His death was a severe blow to French influence in eastern Europe.

Because Alexander's son, Peter, was not of age, a regency was formed under the king's cousin, Prince Paul. Interested chiefly in foreign affairs, Paul entrusted the running of the government to Milan Stojadinović, who remained in office from 1935 to 1939. Meanwhile, the pressure of outside events was growing stronger. In March 1938 Hitler moved into Austria; later in the same year he took the Sudetenland from Czechoslovakia. In this period of emergency, when national unity was urgently needed, Stojadinović was replaced by Dragiša Cvetković, who entered into negotiations with Maček. In August 1939, immediately before the outbreak of World War II, an agreement was signed which granted most of the Croatian demands. An autonomous Croatia was created, which was to control about one fourth of the territory of the Yugoslav state and to have its own assembly and internal administrative system. The central government in Belgrade was to have control over foreign affairs, the army, commerce, and communications; it was to be represented in Croatia by a *ban* (governor). Maček was to hold the position of vice premier in the national government. This arrangement, which failed to satisfy the extremists on both sides, was never given the opportunity to work, because of the immediate outbreak of the war. Once again the fate of the Balkan states was to be determined not by their own decisions but by the acts of the great powers.

International Relations

The political tensions within each state were paralleled by similar conflicts between the Balkan states. The peace treaties and the territorial settlements of World War I had left old quarrels unresolved and had created new ones. These rivalries were thereafter pursued with vigor and, as before, each Balkan government sought the aid of a great power to gain its wishes. The constant international conflicts also justified and made necessary the maintenance of large armies and police forces.

The territorial disputes among the Balkan states remained much the same as before the war. Rumania now held Bessarabia and southern Dobrudja against Soviet and Bulgarian protests; her control of Transylvania, with its large German and Hungarian minorities, embittered relations with these two governments. Yugoslavia disputed her northern frontier with Austria, Italy, and Hungary. Greece had quarrels with Albania, Bulgaria, Turkey, and Yugoslavia—as well as with Britain and Italy—over territorial claims and the treatment of minorities. Bulgaria and Albania were in a worse position. Albania not only had nationals in Greece and Yugoslavia, but she had to fear for her very existence. Bulgaria had lost her share of Thrace and Macedonia and had border disputes with all her neighbors. The existence of these unresolved issues among the Balkan nationals weakened the entire area and allowed the great powers to interfere in their affairs. Between the wars, France, Italy, and then Germany, pursuing a policy of "divide and rule," were able to manipulate events in the Balkans and to organize diplomatic combinations which were to their own advantage.

The first power to exploit the situation was France. Because of her past cultural influence, she enjoyed a great deal of sympathy in the Balkan capitals. After the loss of her prewar ally, tsarist Russia, France sought to replace this power by the creation of an eastern European alliance system which could be used against Germany and the Soviet Union. This policy was a return to the idea of the eastern barrier, by which she had previously sought to unite Poland, Sweden, and the Ottoman Empire against Russia and the Habsburg Empire. Consequently, under French protection, Yugoslavia and Rumania joined with Czechoslovakia to form the Little Entente. The aim of this alliance for the Balkan states was to protect the gains that they had made in the war. Its weakness lay in its dependence upon French arms and on the continued intervention of France in the affairs of central Europe.

The combination of victor states invited the formation of an opposing camp, composed of those who were not satisfied by the territorial settlements of World War I. Italy, in particular, felt that she had been cheated by the peace treaties and, indeed, there was much justification for her grievances. Britain and France had divided between them much enemy territory in Africa and Asia, but they had denied similar claims presented by Italy. In 1922 Benito Mussolini came to power in Italy and soon adopted an openly imperialistic program. First, he endeavored to expand Italian influence in Albania. He also sought closer relations with extremist nationalist groups, such as IMRO in Bulgaria and the Ustaši, a Croatian organization that supported the creation of a separate state. The cooperation with Bulgaria was marked by the marriage of King Boris to Giovanna, the daughter of the king of Italy. Therefore, against the French combination of satisfied states—Czechoslovakia, Yugoslavia, and Rumania—Mussolini placed an alignment of the dissatisfied—Austria, Bulgaria, and Hungary.

Despite the antagonism among the Balkan states, an attempt was made in the 1930s to bring about some sort of regional cooperation. A series of semiofficial conferences was held from 1930 to 1933. In 1934, Greece, Rumania, Turkey, and Yugoslavia signed a treaty of mutual guarantee. Because none of the signatories was willing to see this pact applied against a great power, it became little more than an expression of solidarity in favor of the maintenance of the status quo —which really meant that it was directed against Bulgaria.

In the competition between the two diplomatic systems, it was the French that collapsed first. The Great Depression of the 1930s, which so complicated internal Balkan politics, had an equally destructive effect on foreign affairs. The rise of the Nazi party in Germany, and its assumption of power in 1933, brought that nation back into the Balkan political arena. Balkan resources formed a natural complement to the German industrial plant. Deprived of other markets by the world economic crisis, the Balkan states found themselves increasingly drawn toward Germany. The economic tie was used by Berlin to gain political advantage. As the German position grew stronger, that of France weakened. French military and strategic needs and possibilities had also changed. After the German remilitarization of the Rhineland, the French government proceeded to direct its main military effort toward the construction of a gigantic defensive wall: the Maginot Line. This move signified that in the event of war France could not and would not come to the aid of her eastern allies through an attack on the German western frontier. This military reality doomed the French eastern alliance system.

In 1938 Hitler began to move eastward. The acquisition of Austria proceeded with little difficulty. The German absorption of all of Czechoslovakia in 1939 ended the Little Entente and showed the weakness of the Western powers. The next state to face German pressure was Poland. Determined to stop further German conquests in central Europe, France and Britain gave a guarantee to Poland. In answer to the Polish pact, Hitler—in a dramatic reversal of diplomacy—came to an agreement with Stalin. The two dictators divided Poland between them and Stalin took the Baltic states, Bessarabia, and northern Bukovina. The Soviet Union also agreed to deliver supplies to Germany. On September 1, 1939, the German armies marched into Poland; on September 3rd Britain and France, in accordance with their treaty obligations, declared war, thus inaugurating the second great conflict of the twentieth century.

SEVEN

World War II

The commencement of World War II revived all the great national problems of the Balkans. Despite the fact that the Balkan governments were themselves dictatorships, only Bulgaria could hope to benefit from a German victory. To the other Balkan states, the war situation could only mean danger and disaster.

The German Advance

Albania, as we have seen, had fallen to Italy prior to the beginning of the war. Rumania was the next country to suffer from the consequences of the great European rivalries. Soon after the commencement of the war, the Soviet Union took Bessarabia and northern Bukovina in accordance with the terms of the agreement with Germany. Hungary and Bulgaria, both close to Italy, then presented their claims on Rumanian lands. Germany and Italy, acting as arbiters, in the Vienna Award of 1940 gave southern Dobrudja to Bulgaria and a part of Transylvania to Hungary. Caught between Germany and the Soviet Union, Rumania sought to save the rest of her territory by cooperation with Berlin. King Carol abdicated in favor of his son, Michael, and left the country. The Iron Guard, which had formerly been outlawed, now became the major political organization in the country. Its chief, General Ion Antonescu, was virtual dictator of Rumania through World War II.

Meanwhile, in 1940 the German armies occupied France, and Italy entered the war. When a concentrated air assault on Britain failed to achieve the desired results, Hitler determined upon an attack on the Soviet Union. Until this time the German armies had met with miraculous successes. These achievements were not received with any great enthusiasm by Mussolini, who felt himself, as in 1939, overshadowed by his fellow dictator. Not content with this junior relationship, he decided to gain a great victory on his own. In October 1940, without consulting Hitler, Mussolini delivered an ultimatum to Greece. When it was rejected, he launched an invasion through Albania. Although a quick victory had been expected, the Italian armies were stopped by the Greek forces, which could operate more effectively in the mountainous area of their homeland. The Italian campaign and its failures opened the Balkan area to Allied intervention. Crete was immediately occupied by British soldiers. The rash Italian action thus forced Hitler to turn his attention to the Balkan front. Pressure was put on Bulgaria, which was still officially neutral, to allow the passage of German troops from Rumania to the Greek frontier. In March 1941 Bulgaria joined the Germans and consented to the entrance of German armies. The German government turned next to Yugoslavia. In March 1941 the Yugoslav government signed an agreement with Germany, according to which Yugoslavia was to provide certain military assistance in return for the future possession of territory in Greek Macedonia and the port of Thessaloniki. This capitulation to the German demands provoked an immediate reaction in Belgrade. A military *coup* overthrew the government and brought about the establishment of a new regime under King Peter II. Although the new government tried at first to be neutral, German armies invaded both Yugoslavia and Greece in April. The British landed a few troops in Greece, but the German military action, fast and effective, forced their immediate evacuation. Crete too was subsequently taken by the German forces.

Thus by the summer of 1941, when the German armies began their attack on the Soviet Union, the entire Balkan area was under the control of Germany or her allies and satellites. Yugoslavia, Greece, and Albania were conquered countries; Rumania and Bulgaria were allies. This difference in status was to be of great political significance later. Once again, however, the Balkan states were in no position to control their own future. Their fate now depended upon that of the German campaign in the Soviet Union. A quick German victory in this field would preclude any effective Balkan action.

The Resistance Movements

The failure of the German armies to gain their major military objectives and their slow withdrawal from the Soviet Union gave the Balkan nations the opportunity to play an important military role in the war through the resistance movements organized in Axis-occupied regions. These activities, moreover, soon came to have far more than a military significance. Throughout the Balkans the resistance organizations reflected the political divisions of the countries concerned. The conservative, or Right-wing, groups were led by those who had been in power before the war and they naturally favored a re-establishment of prewar conditions. The organizations on the Left advocated thorough reform or even a revolutionary change in the government. The most active and effective forces were generally those formed from the political Left, and within these the Communists were able to gain a controlling position. Because the more radical resistance groups did the most damage to the enemy, the Allies also favored them and gave them material support. For instance, in Yugoslavia Tito's forces received more military assistance than did the followers of Mihailović, who represented the prewar government.

The Allies' wartime policy of supporting those partisan groups who were doing the most fighting was based on the premise that the most important consideration was to win the war. Problems of postwar reorganization were to be solved later. The result of this decision was that at the end of the war the armed power in each region was in the hands of the Communist-dominated resistance forces. During their initial victories in the Balkans, the Germans had either destroyed or made allies of the regular Balkan armies. These forces had previously been the chief military support of the regimes in power. Thereafter in Yugoslavia, Greece, and Albania, the resistance forces constituted the strongest national troops. At the end of the war the regular Bulgarian and Rumanian armies, being enemy organizations, were disarmed and taken over by the victorious Russian armies. The small, Left-oriented resistance forces, with backing from the Soviet armies, were then able to dominate the states.

The war thus brought about a complete shift in the political structure in each Balkan state. Before the war the army had controlled or been controlled by the regime in power; the Communists and the other parties of the Left had been suppressed. After 1939 the German armies became the instrument by which the military power of the old regimes was destroyed. The Communists, who had a program of action and who had great experience in underground activity, subsequently took the lead in organizing resistance movements. These groups included not only those who agreed with Communist principles, but also many who wished to pursue vigorous and active policies against the invaders. These organizations received substantial Allied aid and, later, the presence of the Soviet armies further strengthened their position. Thus during the war the foundation was laid for the introduction of a new political system into the Balkans.

BULGARIA. Bulgaria and Rumania, as countries allied with Germany and Italy, had the weakest resistance movements. Bulgaria also suffered less than the other Balkan countries in the war. Unlike Rumania, she refused to send troops to fight in the Soviet Union, arguing that her people were too pro-Russian to allow this participation. Because she was allied to Germany, she, of course, did not have to submit to an Axis occupation. As her part in the war, her troops did guard duty in Thrace, in Macedonia, and in parts of Serbia. Nevertheless, a resistance movement under Communist sponsorship, the Fatherland Front, was formed by the parties of the Left. They opposed the dictatorship of the king and they did not want a German victory. As in the other countries, guerrilla bands operated in the mountains, but they did not gain wide support because the land was not suffering under really acute war conditions. In 1943 King Boris died and, because his son was not of age, his brother, Prince Cyril, became regent. Cyril's increasingly pro-German actions added to the popularity of the resistance. In May 1944, as the Soviet armies approached, the partisans were able to take over the government. The military power they lacked was soon supplied by the Soviet army.

RUMANIA. Unlike Bulgaria, Rumania actively participated on the side of the Axis and incurred heavy losses. At the beginning of the war much territory had been surrendered to the Soviet Union, Hungary, and Bulgaria; many soldiers were also lost in the war in the Soviet Union. Of all of the Balkan countries, Rumania had the smallest and least important resistance movement. In the other states, the Russians had enjoyed a certain degree of popularity because of their role in the liberation of the peninsula from Ottoman rule and because of past associations of religion or race. These feelings had been carried over into the Soviet era despite the many changes that had occurred within the Russian state. To many, the name *Russia* was still associated with concepts of national liberation. Moreover, the Soviet Union, because of her own weaknesses and difficulties, had been unable to exert influence or domination in the Balkans in the interwar period. Soviet assistance during the war seemed the only hope against German conquest. These feelings toward the Soviet Union, however, were not common in Rumania. The problem of Bessarabia and the more indefinite feeling of Slavic encirclement had a strong influence on the general attitude. In 1943 the Communists were able to form a front organization of the Left, but it remained very weak. In Rumania, more than in any other Balkan state, the presence of the Soviet army and direct Soviet intervention was necessary to bring about the victory of the Communist forces.

ALBANIA. In contrast to Rumania, Albania had an active and effective partisan organization: the National Liberation Front. Its leader was Enver Hoxha, who worked closely with and obtained aid from Tito. Thus from the beginning the Albanian movement was closely linked with that in Yugoslavia. Although there were other Albanian resistance groups, it was the National Liberation Front which, at the end of the war, had military control of the country and had also set up an administrative system.

YUGOSLAVIA. Because of the strategic importance of Yugoslavia and Greece, the resistance movements in these countries were of the greatest significance both for the winning of the war and for the postwar division of the Balkans. The most effective and active of all of the partisan movements was that organized in Yugoslavia, where the terrain and the long tradition of guerrilla warfare contributed to the success of the action. Immediately after the German occupation, the Axis powers undertook the reorganization of the country. Slovenia was divided between Germany and Italy; Hungary took Baranja, Bačka, and part of Croatia; Bulgaria occupied the Yugoslav sections of Macedonia; Italy held Montenegro, Dalmatia, and a part of Bosnia-Hercegovina; an Albanian government was set up in the Kosovo-Metohija area. Croatia was given a separate organization and made a dependency of Italy. The political control within Croatia was held by the Ustaši under Ante Pavelić. Serbia, reduced to its pre-Balkan War size, was under German occupation. Its administration was entrusted to General Milan Nedić and to those Serbs who were willing to collaborate with Germany. Within the country as a whole, political and military confusion and chaos ruled. In Croatia the hitherto submerged forces of Croatian nationalism now found themselves in control. Throughout the country, Catholics and Moslems turned on Orthodox and Jews. The German occupation policies and the reprisals taken against the population, together with the breakdown of internal order, created ideal conditions for the rise of a resistance movement. Many were left with the alternative of joining the partisan bands or being massacred.

Because it was bound to a military timetable for the Russian campaign, the German army was not able to disarm all the units of the Yugoslav army. A resistance movement, the Chetniks, under General Draža Mihailović, was thus able to form almost at once. This group, dominated by Serbs and supporting the former government, suffered from the beginning from problems of organization and from its limited social and national appeal. The stronger force became that established by the political groups of the Left under the Communist leader, Josip Broz Tito. This movement, centered in the mountainous area of Bosnia, benefited from its leaders' experience in underground operations. Tito's support of a federal Yugoslav state also won him many adherents. The two partisan bands, organized along different political and national lines, soon came into conflict. A three-sided war thus developed between the Chetniks, Tito's partisans, and the occupation forces. Tito's continual harassment of the enemy, with little or no regard for the danger of reprisals, made his movement the more popular with the Allies. Britain at this time played the chief role in the making of Allied policy in both Yugoslavia and Greece. The Soviet Union was fully occupied in its own country; the United States, in general, followed British advice. Under British guidance, the Allies considered the problem of resistance primarily from the military standpoint; both Yugoslav resistance leaders, in contrast, were thinking of the future. Mihailović was also the minister of war in the Yugoslav government-in-exile in London. His group naturally feared that the Communists would dominate postwar Yugoslavia. Convinced that the Germans were bound to be defeated and fearing that Yugoslavia would then be Communist, the Chetnik forces began to cooperate with the armies of occupation and to operate against the partisans. In this situation—and again considering only the immediate military situation—the Allies withdrew their assistance from the government-in-exile and gave their support only to Tito's forces. In 1944, the German armies were forced to evacuate Yugoslavia. When the Soviet armies entered Belgrade, they found that the partisans had military control of the country and had set up an administrative system. The first postwar government in Yugoslavia, like those established in other Balkan states, was based on the cooperation of all of the parties of the Left.

GREECE. Like Yugoslavia, Greece suffered from the extremely harsh conditions of the occupation. The Albanians administered Epirus; the Bulgarians held Thrace and Macedonia. The rest of the country was under German and Italian control, wielded through a puppet government established in Athens. Economic conditions were particularly bad after the Germans stripped the country of supplies they needed for the Russian campaign. Because the Greeks must import 50 per cent of their food, the interruption of this supply produced famine conditions throughout the nation. During the war years, about 30 per cent of the national wealth of Greece and about 7 per cent of the population was destroyed. Conditions in Greece, like those in Yugoslavia, were thus propitious for the rise of partisan movements. The strongest of these, the National Liberation Front (EAM), the equivalent of Tito's partisans, included Left and Center groups as well as others who wished to carry on an active policy against the occupying powers. Greece, like Yugoslavia, had a government-in-exile. Its military force was the Greek National Democratic League (EDES), under the direction of General Zervas. In December 1942 EAM established a military organization known as the National Popular Party of Liberation (ELAS). Thereafter it organized and carried through military actions, much as Tito's forces did. The Allies gave it similar assistance. Unlike Tito's partisans, however, the Greek resistance of the Left did not break its ties with the government-in-exile, which at first had its headquarters in Egypt. Thus, at the end of the war, although EAM had control of the strongest military forces and had organized an administration in the territory it controlled, it continued to regard the government-in-exile as the legal administrator of the country. Moreover, it sought to join this government and to influence its decisions. The break between the government forces and the resistance came only in December 1944. This event was the prelude to a long and bloody civil war.

At the end of World War II, therefore, Albania, Greece, and Yugoslavia were under the control of the resistance movements dominated by the Left. Bulgaria and Rumania, former Axis allies, were given similar regimes under the protection of the Soviet army. It should be emphasized that the Left enjoyed a great prestige among the Balkan peoples after the war because of its active and aggressive role in the struggle against the German invading forces. The final decision on the political and territorial disposition of Balkan affairs, however, now as in the past, depended not on the people concerned but upon the relations between the great powers. Unfortunately for the Balkans, the victor powers, like all wartime coalitions, split after the war and quarreled among themselves. It was in a dispute over Balkan affairs that the great postwar political division between the Western powers and the Soviet bloc was first to be clearly shown.

EIGHT

Since World War II

Soviet Postwar Predominance

In terms of power politics, the Soviet Union had the advantage at the end of the hostilities in Europe. Not only were Soviet armies in occupation of Bulgaria and Rumania, but within each state Communist-led resistance movements held the principal political power. In Greece, Yugoslavia, and Albania, the partisans also had effective military units. The situation had now been created in the Balkans which both British and Habsburg diplomacy had so long labored to prevent in the nineteenth century. Moreover a great difference in aims and methods separated the Russia of the tsars from the Soviet Union of Stalin. Nineteenth-century Russia generally sought to preserve the status quo in foreign affairs and in domestic policy. Her religious and racial ties with the Balkan peoples brought her repeatedly into the affairs of the peninsula. The Balkan states, as we have seen, were liberated chiefly by the force of Russian arms. Once rid of Ottoman domination, however, these nations were usually able to remain free of direct Russian control and they adopted forms of government modeled after those of the liberal West. Tsarist Russia did not insist upon ideological conformity, and tsarism itself was not a doctrine for export. The Bolshevik Revolution brought a temporary end to Russian influence. For the entire interwar period, the Soviet Union played a smaller role in Balkan affairs than did the other great powers. Moreover, Soviet power was contained by the existence of a strong Japan in the east and the rise of Nazi Germany in the west. These states, which had acted as barriers against Soviet influence, were completely eliminated at the end of the war. The Soviet Union thereafter emerged as the single strong nation bordering on an area weakened by years of war and political controversy. No power was willing or able to block the advance of Soviet influence into eastern Europe. The United States, after the conclusion of the actual fighting, showed a strong desire to withdraw from Europe as soon as possible. American troops were sent home and the wartime economic aid ceased.

The Soviet Union was more than a state faced with a fine opportunity to increase its power; it was also a revolutionary regime of a type unknown in Europe since the French Revolution. Unlike tsarist Russia, the Soviet Union did have a doctrine for export; it was one which was not only considered morally right, but whose ultimate victory was believed inevitable. Convinced of the deep and basic antagonism between the "capitalist, imperialist" nations and the socialist states, the Soviet government looked upon its wartime allies with increasing suspicion and distrust. The reorganization of the central and southeastern European governments, the creation of so-called "friendly regimes," was regarded as essential for the security of the Soviet Union as well as for the advancement of Communism.

With considerable experience in eastern affairs, Britain's attitude was more realistic than that of the United States. In order to forestall complete Soviet domination of the Balkans, the British prime minister, Winston Churchill, sought to make some kind of an arrangement with the Soviet Union before the end of the war. In 1944 he came to an agreement with Stalin on the establishment of spheres of interest in the Balkans. The Soviet Union was to be allowed predominant control in Rumania and Bulgaria; Britain was to determine policy in Greece; Yugoslavia was to be split between the two. This division of the Balkans, to which the United States did not adhere, was replaced by the Yalta Declaration of February 1945, which called for the formation of "interim governmental authorities broadly representative of all democratic elements in the population and pledged to the earliest possible establishment, through free elections, of governments responsive to the will of the people." Despite its signature to this agreement, the Soviet Union thereafter pressed for the establishment of purely Communist regimes throughout eastern Europe and freely employed methods other than "free elections" for the accomplishment of this aim.

The assumption of full power by Tito's adherents in Yugoslavia was facilitated by the fact that the Communists were in effective control of the country at the end of the war. Under the prompting of the West, Tito at first agreed to include in his government some representatives of the government-in-exile and some prewar political leaders, but by January 1946 he had taken complete control—and without Soviet assistance. The situation in Rumania and Bulgaria was, in contrast, more complex. The Soviet Union first dealt with the governments in power, which were not in Communist hands. Both countries had also been allied with Germany and had participated in the Axis military ventures. Here the presence of the Soviet military forces determined the final political form of the governments.

In August 1944 the approach of the Soviet armies and the imminent German collapse forced Rumania to change allegiance. Taking an active stand, King Michael, who had replaced his father in 1940, declared war on Germany. Thereafter the Rumanian troops fought with the Soviet Union. The presence of Soviet military forces in the country led almost immediately to a change in the government. In March 1945, under strong Soviet pressure, the king accepted a Communist-dominated cabinet. Although the United States at first protested, the western Allies finally recognized the new regime. The Communist control of the government assured a victory in the next elections, which were held in November 1946. In 1947 King Michael abdicated; in the following year an assembly under full Communist control drew up a constitution.

Events in Bulgaria followed much the same course, although that country, even in alliance with Germany, had never declared war on the Soviet Union. The Rumanian shift to the Soviet side in August 1944 placed Bulgaria in an impossible military situation. The government therefore turned to the western Allies in an attempt to make peace. Fearing that this move would lead to a diminution of its future influence in the country, the Soviet Union declared war and Soviet troops entered Bulgaria. Under Soviet military sponsorship, the Fatherland Front set up a coalition government composed of those groups which had opposed Bulgarian cooperation with the Axis. The Communists held four cabinet posts, including the ministries of the interior and of justice. Bulgarian troups now joined the Soviet armies. Unlike Rumania, Bulgaria received relatively lenient treatment from the occupying power. She was not required to pay huge reparations to the Soviet Union, and she was allowed to keep southern Dobrudja, formerly a part of Rumania. Gradually full control of the government was taken by the Communist party. Opposition leaders were forced to flee or were imprisoned. By August 1948 Communist domination in Bulgaria was fully established.

The Communist victory in Bulgaria, Yugoslavia, Rumania, and Albania was paralleled by a similar course of events in Poland, East Germany, Hungary, and Czechoslovakia. It appeared at the time that Greece too might fall to the Soviet bloc. The West was thus faced with a new diplomatic situation. Because Britain and France could not meet the new threat alone, the United States was forced to return to active participation in European politics and, at great cost, to rebuild the barriers which had been broken down. The former enemies, Germany and Japan, were given economic aid and a great system of military alliances was developed to form a wall against further Soviet expansion.

The New Alliances

The formation of the two new European alliance systems began soon after the end of the war. In 1946 Stalin named the western Allies as the enemies of his country; in 1947 in a speech in the United States, Churchill described the "iron curtain" that was being drawn across Europe. In the same year the Truman Doctrine was proclaimed for the protection of Greece and Turkey. The Communist triumph in China in 1949 emphasized the need for unity in the West. The principal alliance upon which Western defense came to be based, the North Atlantic Treaty Organization (NATO), was formed in 1949. Its original members were Britain, the United States, France, the Netherlands, Luxembourg, Denmark, Iceland, Norway, Italy, Portugal, and Canada. Greece and Turkey joined in 1951; West Germany, in 1955. In addition to these military arrangements, the United States—through the Marshall Plan of 1948—offered economic assistance to its allies and to the states associated with them.

The economic and military alignment of the West was balanced by similar associations formed among the Soviet-bloc nations. After the war the Soviet Union negotiated a series of bilateral pacts with the states in her political orbit. In 1949, in reply to the Marshall Plan, the Council for Mutual Economic Assistance (COMECON) was established. In 1955 the Warsaw Pact was signed by Albania, Bulgaria, Czechoslovakia, East Germany, Hungary, Poland, Rumania, and the Soviet Union. The two alliance systems described here set the diplomatic pattern for the Balkan peninsula as well as for Europe. It is within this framework that the events of the postwar years must be considered.

Balkan Socialism and the Prewar Communist Parties

It has already been shown how, in the nineteenth century, the newly liberated Balkan states took as their pattern of government that introduced into Europe through the French Revolution and supported thereafter in general by the Liberal parties. After World War II another Western doctrine, Marxism, became the revolutionary ideology. The socialist movements in the Balkans began in the nineteenth century, but their development was slow. Because of the low level of industrial growth, the Balkans lacked an organized, class-conscious working class which could form the basis of an effective socialist movement. Moreover, the workers usually remained closely attached to their peasant origins and to their villages. Like his European counterpart, the Balkan socialist had a choice between the program of those who favored an evolutionary means of establishing a socialist state and those who wished to achieve victory through revolution. The more militant joined the Communist parties formed after World War I. The leadership of the socialist movement lay in the hands of the middle-class intellectuals, but elements of the peasantry and the working class were represented too.

YUGOSLAVIA. In the period after World War I, the Communist party of Yugoslavia showed considerable strength. In the elections of 1920, it received 200,000 votes and thus gained fifty-eight seats, about fourteen per cent of the assembly. The government, however, prevented the Communist deputies from taking their seats. Outlawed in 1921, the party thereafter went underground. A small Socialist party was allowed to continue, but it attracted little support. The Yugoslav Communist party remained closely associated with Moscow until 1925, when it broke with the Soviet Union. It was not until 1937, when Tito assumed leadership, that the party again became active and effective.

BULGARIA. In Bulgaria, as in Yugoslavia, the Communist party was able to gain many votes in the first elections after World War I. In 1919 it had one fifth of the seats in the Bulgarian assembly and, with the agrarians, commanded the majority of the votes. The two parties of the Left, however, did not cooperate. When Stamboliski was overthrown in June 1923, the Communists did nothing to aid his party. When the Communists belatedly staged a *coup* in September, they were easily put down. In 1924, after much bloodshed and many imprisonments, the Communist party was banned. Thereafter, it attempted to use terrorist methods. The most spectacular of these was the blowing up of the cathedral in Sofia, a disaster which caused the death of 125 people. Although the Communist party itself was illegal, a front organization—the Workers' Party—was formed in 1927. In 1935, when general Communist policy resulted in the participation of the party in political combinations with other groups, the Bulgarian Communists cooperated with other opponents of the government. In 1936, the opposition to the king won sixty-three out of the 160 assembly seats. It is not possible to determine how many of these deputies were elected by the Communists. The Bulgarian Communist party was, nevertheless, the strongest in the Balkans.

RUMANIA. In contrast, the Rumanian Communist party, founded in 1921, remained weak. Outlawed by the Liberal government in 1927, it continued to carry on underground activities and to play a part in the political life of the country until 1933. After that time, the government of King Carol made a concerted effort to destroy it. This endeavor was continued with even greater intensity during World War II, when Rumania fought with Germany against the Soviet Union. Thus when the Soviet armies arrived in Rumania, they found few genuine Communist partisans.

GREECE. The Communist party of Greece, although more significant than that of Rumania, did not approach in strength those of Bulgaria or of Yugoslavia in the interwar period. Throughout these years the party was greatly hampered by the support given by general Communist policy to the idea of the creation of an independent Macedonian state. The proposed dismemberment of the country through the detachment of Greek Macedonia was not likely to win much enthusiasm, particularly after the disastrous campaign in Turkey. In 1936 the Greek Communists formed part of a Popular Front which won fifteen seats and held the balance between two larger factions which were evenly divided in strength. It was this situation which led to the dictatorship of Metaxas, who thereafter justified many of his repressive measures by citing the danger of Communism. When Metaxas abolished all political parties, the Communists went underground.

Because the Communists operated illegally during most of the interwar period, it is difficult to assess their strength at that time. No doubt many joined the party in protest against the dictatorial character of the governments in power rather than through belief in Communist doctrine. It can, however, be safely estimated that the Communists were a small minority in all of the Balkan countries. Had it not been for World War II, which gave them military and political power and won them Soviet support, there is little chance that they could so swiftly have gained control of the government through normal electoral procedures.

Communist Policies

With the Communist party in power in Yugoslavia, Rumania, Bulgaria, and Albania, the states became closely associated with the other socialist states: Czechoslovakia, East Germany, Hungary, and Poland. Although this bloc almost at once developed internal tensions, the political evolution of all its members was similar. The Balkan states demonstrate this development clearly. Of first importance in each country was the Communist party's assumption of absolute dominance over the political apparatus. The other political parties were suppressed; their leaders either joined the new regime or were imprisoned, executed, or exiled. In the elections only Communist or Communist-approved candidates appeared on the ballots. Criticism, although allowed and even encouraged within the party, could not be directed against the regime itself or the new leaders. Newspapers and other media of mass communication were strictly controlled. Internal opposition was either eliminated or discouraged through purges, highly publicized trials, and the continual subjection of the population to massive propaganda campaigns. To replace the former leaders, a new elite of Communist party officials, bureaucrats, experts, and military men now came into being.

Once in firm control, the Communist leaders proceeded to put into effect their political and economic program. The major resources of the state were thereafter devoted to a great attempt at industrialization. The goal was to change the agrarian economies of the backward Balkan states into something more closely resembling those of the more advanced industrial societies. Private ownership and direction were largely abolished; all sections of the national economy were put under the direct control of the government. Primary emphasis was placed upon the building up of the basic industrial plants rather than upon the production of consumer goods. At first each country attempted to follow the pattern of the Soviet Union and to develop independent and complete industrial units. Within the Soviet bloc, East Germany and Czechoslovakia already had a good industrial base. Agrarian Bulgaria, Yugoslavia, and Rumania now followed a similar program, despite their lack of many essential resources.

Through rigid control and state planning, the new regimes were able to achieve a great increase in industrial capacity. The process was made more difficult because of the initial lack of experienced managers and trained and skilled workers, a weakness which still exists throughout the Balkans. The effort put into the construction of great industries also made necessary a low standard of living for the general population. This condition, which deprived the workers of a material incentive to increase their productivity, adversely affected industrial development. The drive toward industrialization is reflected in every aspect of the national life of the socialist states. The emphasis on industry has led naturally to a great increase in the number of those employed in this sector of the economy, and the size of the Balkan towns has altered accordingly. The effects can be clearly seen in the new architecture, the clothing of the people, and the general type of consumer goods available.

In contrast to the accomplishments in industry, the agricultural program has been a comparative failure. According to Communist theory, the ideal solution for the land problem is the abolition of private ownership and the organization of agricultural production along the lines of industry, with the peasant occupying a position comparable to that of a factory worker. As a first step toward this goal, the Communist regimes enforced collectivization upon the peasant land-holder. It was believed that the larger units formed by the pooling of many small plots would also make scientific, mechanized farming possible and practical and that larger yields could then be obtained from the land. The agricultural program, however, suffered from the fact that the governments of the socialist countries put very little effort into it. Investment in the agricultural sector of the economy remained much lower than that in industry. Adequate machinery, tools, and chemicals were not made available. Moreover, the peasant farmer did not work well on the collective farms. Despite all efforts made to persuade him to the contrary, the worker on the land remained attached to the principle of private ownership; he did not wish to be a member of a rural proletariat. In Yugoslavia collectivization was eventually abandoned. Agriculture remains the great weakness of the economies of all of the Balkan socialist states.

The Balkan States in International Affairs

It has been shown how postwar conditions brought about the establishment of Communist-dominated governments in four of the five Balkan states. These regimes came to power in close association with, and under the protection of, the Soviet Union, giving that country clear political predominance in eastern Europe after World War II. In the first years of their existence, the socialist governments followed strictly Soviet patterns of politics and economics and accepted Soviet leadership in foreign affairs. The tightness of the relations within the socialist bloc increased after the defection of one member: Yugoslavia. It was only after Stalin's death in 1953, and Khrushchev's denunciation of Stalinism in 1956, that a real alteration in the attitude of the Eastern European states toward the Soviet Union was possible. Yugoslavia had repudiated Soviet control in 1948; after 1956 a similar reaction occurred in Poland, Hungary, Albania, and Rumania, although the protests took different forms and achieved varying degrees of success. The two factors of polycentrism and revisionism—involving the demand by the Communist parties of the socialist states that they be freed of the domination of the Communist party of the Soviet Union—resulted in a basic change in the relationship between these states and the Soviet Union. Because of these events, and also because of the Communist failure in the Greek civil war, the Soviet position in the Balkans by the 1960s was considerably weaker than it had been immediately after the close of World War II.

GREECE. Although Communist-dominated regimes had been established in Albania, Bulgaria, Rumania, and Yugoslavia by the end of 1945, the political fate of Greece remained in doubt until as late as 1949. The problem in this country was complicated by the prewar political events. The wartime government-in-exile was a continuation of the unpopular Metaxas dictatorship. Moreover, as a result of the war four fifths of the territory of Greece was under the control of EAM/ELAS, in which the Communists—although a minority—had the most powerful position. This group, as has been mentioned, sought not to destroy the legal government, but to join it.

Immediately prior to the liberation of Greece, a moderate coalition cabinet under George Papandreou was formed with representatives from all parties. It was agreed that the armed forces of the partisans and the government-in-exile should be put under the single command of the government. A plebiscite was to be held later to decide if the king should be allowed to return. In October 1944 the government-in-exile came back to Athens under the protection of British troops. It has been estimated that at this time EAM/ELAS had about 40,000 troops; the government forces were about 10,000; and the British, 400. The Leftist organizations thus had a clear military superiority. The policy of cooperation between the government and EAM did not last long. Once in Athens, the government attempted to gain control of all the armed forces and to disarm EAM/ELAS. In December the EAM members left the cabinet in protest and called for a general strike. During this action the police fired upon the crowds and a civil war broke out. The British immediately rushed in troops to handle the situation. The civil conflict ended with the agreement of Varkiza in February 1945. It was agreed that the defeated EAM would surrender its arms and that a plebiscite would be held on the question of the restoration of the monarchy, to be followed by the elections for the assembly. Despite this pact, EAM did not give up all its arms, but hid them for future use.

Immediately a strong Rightist reaction took place. Great numbers of former EAM/ELAS members found themselves in jail on very weak charges. Right and Left extremist groups increased in power and the feeling on both sides became more intense. The British, under great criticism from abroad for their intervention in the civil strife, attempted to secure the formation of a stable national government as soon as possible. It was decided that the elections should be held before the plebiscite on the return of the king. The elections of December 1945 were carried out under bad general circumstances. The entire EAM abstained. The Greek voter was not given a real opportunity to choose between a republic, a monarchy, and a socialist government. As one account states: "The Greek elector was faced with the choice of voting for parties which were prepared to accept the monarchy or abstaining altogether."[1]

---

[1] Bickham Sweet-Escott, *Greece: A Political and Economic Survey, 1939-1953* (London: Royal Institute of International Affairs, 1954), p. 54.

After the elections, a government under Constantine Tsaldaris was formed and the plebiscite was held earlier than had been planned. Receiving 65 per cent of the vote, George II returned to Greece. When he died, his brother, Paul, came to the throne. Because the political struggle had been won by the Right, the Left now prepared to resort to civil war once more. Guerrilla activity increased in the countryside and it became clear that aid was being sent from Albania, Bulgaria, and Yugoslavia. At this point the British government turned to the United States for assistance. In March 1947 the Truman Doctrine was formulated; its purpose was to defend Greece and Turkey from Communist domination. Soviet influence was still strong in Belgrade, and a victory by the Greek rebels would have brought the entire Balkan area into the Soviet sphere. Control of the eastern Mediterranean was also at issue. Aid—both military and economic—was sent by the United States. By 1963 about $3.5 billion had been given to Greece. The shift of the burden of the defense of the eastern Mediterranean from Britain to the United States was a major diplomatic event. For the first time, the United States entered actively into the struggle for the control of the Balkan peninsula.

The Greek civil war lasted from 1946 to 1949. At first the rebels were greatly aided by the fact that they could cross easily the frontiers of the neighboring states. They were also able to establish control over the greater part of Greece. The government forces, however, had the aid of the United States, which supplied much war material and retrained the Greek army. Two other events also helped the government. First, in 1948 Yugoslavia broke with the Soviet Union and in 1949 closed her border to the Greek rebels. Second, the Cominform, an organization of Soviet-bloc states formed in 1947, endorsed the creation of an independent Macedonian state as a move against Yugoslavia. Because such a state would also include Greek, or Aegean, Macedonia, a rebel victory appeared to involve a dismemberment of Greece.

By the winter of 1949-50 the conflict had ended. It left behind great internal problems and general devastation. The West had, nevertheless, kept the strategically important area within its sphere. Although the Communist party was outlawed in Greece, the Left remained politically active through a union party, the United Democratic Left (EDA), which won a quarter of the seats in the Greek assembly in 1958. This number, however, fell to only 11 per cent in 1964.

Despite the victory of the government and the end of the civil war, one issue remained as a threat to the peace in the eastern Mediterranean: the question of the island of Cyprus. Although Greece and Turkey were both members of the NATO alliance, these two historic enemies were at odds over the fate of the island. Cyprus had been acquired by Britain from the Ottoman Empire in 1878 as compensation for Russian gains in Bulgaria and in the Caucasus. The population of the island is about 80 per cent Greek and 20 per cent Turkish, but it lies forty miles from Turkey and 600 miles from the Greek mainland. After World War II, the Greek population demanded an end to British rule and union with Greece; the Turkish minority countered with a demand for the partition of the island. Finally, after much bloodshed, it was agreed that the island would be formed into an independent republic under the joint protection of Britain, Turkey, and Greece. The constitution of the new state provided strong safeguards for the rights of the Turkish minority. Despite this change, the problem remained unsolved because of the continuing friction between the Greek and Turkish elements. In 1964 another crisis forced the sending of United Nations troops to the island.

YUGOSLAVIA. The defection of Yugoslavia from the Soviet camp was another great gain for the West. After the war the Communist party of Yugoslavia was in a very strong position. The partisans had won their victories without any significant Soviet aid; the supplies and equipment brought in from abroad had been chiefly British or American. The Yugoslav Communist officials were self-confident and proud of their achievements. As could be expected, friction soon developed with the Soviet officials who arrived after the war. Although they recognized that the liberation of their country had been made possible because of the Soviet victories over the German armies, the Yugoslav leaders did not see this as a reason why their national life should be submitted to Soviet control. A number of incidents occurred between the two countries. By 1948 an open break had taken place. In March, Tito and Stalin exchanged a series of letters bitterly accusing each other of ideological deviation and of misdeeds in connection with military and economic matters. In June 1948 the matter was discussed by the socialist states at a Cominform meeting. In a resolution dated June 28th, the anniversary of the battle of Kosovo and the assassination of Franz Ferdinand, the Cominform members called upon the Yugoslav Communists to force their government to change its policy or to replace it "and to advance a new international leadership of the party." This last statement was an open invitation to revolution. It was after this meeting that the March correspondence between the two leaders was published. In July the Communist Party of Yugoslavia held its fifth congress. In a nine-hour speech, Tito defended his position and denounced that of the Soviet Union. The first break in the postwar Communist bloc had taken place; the question remained whether Tito was strong enough to maintain his defiant attitude.

Immediately after this challenge to Soviet influence, the Soviet Union and the states associated with her took measures against Yugoslavia. The Albanians seized the opportunity to throw off the Yugoslav influence and control which had been established in their country. The radio and press of all the socialist-bloc countries launched violent attacks against the Yugoslav leadership and support was given to anti-Tito emigrant Yugoslav groups. Many border incidents occurred. As might have been expected, socialist-bloc commercial and financial arrangements with Belgrade were broken. Finally, in September and October 1949, all the Cominform states ended their pacts of mutual assistance with Yugoslavia. In the same year Tito closed his border with Greece, thus cutting off any further effective assistance to the Greek rebels. Tito's actions also influenced the internal affairs of the other socialist countries. The governments of these countries used the opportunity to conduct purges of opposition elements and those who criticized Soviet domination.

Although the real issue in the Yugoslav-Soviet dispute was the national independence of a socialist state and its right to follow its own road to socialism, the quarrel was conducted in public on other principles. To justify their position, the Yugoslavs now attempted to show that they were better Marxists and truer Communists than those in the Soviet Union, which, they argued, was an example of state capitalism and not communism. In an effort to find an effective and unique counterdoctrine, they put forward the idea of the Workers' Councils. In January 1950, it was decided that the workers in each industrial unit would elect councils of between fifteen and 120 members; from these a management board would be chosen. The councils would run the factories and determine such questions as the price of the goods produced and the hours and conditions of work. In theory, this plan gave the direction of the factories to the workers; it also introduced a needed incentive because the factories could win profits for the members. The competitive principle was also put into effect between factories. The establishment of Workers' Councils was paralleled by an attempt at decentralization and by reforms in other sections of the government. In 1953 collectivization was abandoned and the peasants were allowed to withdraw their property from the system. It should be emphasized that these changes in no way weakened the political dominance of the Communist party in the state. It remained the central controlling influence, but a greater degree of flexibility was introduced into economic life.

Despite her first successes in withstanding outside pressure, Yugoslavia now stood militarily and economically isolated, a position she could not long maintain. The break with Moscow made possible a renewal of ties with the West. Although Tito refused to compromise his political beliefs, he did need assistance. In December 1948, Yugoslavia entered into trade agreements with Britain; in 1949 the United States allowed the Yugoslav government to buy aircraft and aviation gasoline. The Yugoslav economic situation, however, was gravely compromised by the drought of 1950. At that time the United States agreed to give $75 million in assistance. Yugoslavia was also offered military aid and she obtained further financial support from international organizations. By 1963 over $2.5 billion in the form of aid, loans, and credit had been received from the United States alone. Yugoslavia's shift toward the West went even further in 1953, when she signed a pact of friendship and cooperation with Greece and Turkey. In 1954 this agreement was strengthened by an agreement providing for reciprocal aid should any of the three states be attacked by another power. Yugoslavia also settled her dispute with Italy over Trieste. Although still a socialist state, Yugoslavia by this time had come to rely on the West for military support and economic assistance.

Another change in the Yugoslav position occurred after the death of Stalin in 1953, an event which brought about great changes in the Soviet Union and in the relations among the socialist-bloc states. Khrushchev's repudiation of Stalin made possible an improvement of relations with Yugoslavia. In 1955 the Soviet leader visited Tito and, in effect, admitted the error of his country's former stand. In 1956, the Twentieth Party Congress of the Soviet Communist party recognized that different roads to socialism were possible and that all states need not adhere rigidly to the Soviet pattern. Inasmuch as this had been their argument all along, the Yugoslavs felt that their program had received full justification. It was the Soviet party, not the Yugoslav, which had changed. In 1956, in a further step in the same direction, the Cominform was disbanded.

The Soviet repudiation of Stalinism and the successful Yugoslav resistance to pressure had a great effect in the other Soviet-bloc states, particularly in Poland and Hungary. In 1956, Poland, under the leadership of Gomulka, succeeded in breaking away from tight Russian control. Greater freedom was allowed in internal political and cultural life, and an exchange of students and professors with the United States was begun. In Hungary, in contrast, the move toward more independence led to disaster. The revolution which took place in 1956 was put down by the Soviet army; the Hungarian premier, Imre Nagy, was executed. The events in Poland showed what the Soviet Union would tolerate; the Hungarian Revolution, which called for the removal of Communist rule altogether, was too great a challenge to Soviet power to remain unanswered.

Despite the re-establishment of relations with the Soviet Union, Yugoslavia did not return to the Soviet camp. Instead, Tito continued to play a delicate balancing act between the two great power alignments. He did not wish to give up American military and economic aid, but Yugoslavia was a socialist country and thus linked politically with the states with similar regimes. In order to strengthen his own position, Tito joined with other nations in an attempt to form a third, "neutralist" bloc. He cooperated chiefly with the leaders of the three great nonaligned nations: Nasser of the United Arab Republic, Nehru of India, and Sukarno of Indonesia. The four political leaders hoped that, by working together, they would constitute a real force in world affairs and be in a position to accept assistance from both East and West. They tried also to appeal to other Asian and African countries that were in a similar position.

ALBANIA. The third, and perhaps the least expected, of the major postwar developments in the Balkans took place in Albania. After World War II Albania had no sooner been freed of Italian rule than she fell under Yugoslav influence. The Albanian Communist party was led by Enver Hoxha, a French-educated Moslem Tosk of middle-class background. Although postwar Albania had a socialist regime, it was so completely under Yugoslav domination that it did not even have a place in the Cominform. The Albanian economy was also under Yugoslav control. In 1947, 58 per cent of the state income was from Yugoslav credits. The close association of the two governments again faced Albania with the possibility of being absorbed by a larger neighbor.

In these circumstances, the Tito-Stalin controversy offered Albania a welcome opportunity for breaking the Yugoslav hold. She therefore strongly supported the Soviet position. In 1949 Koci Xoxe, a rival of Hoxha, was executed as a "Titoist." Yugoslav economic assistance was replaced with aid from the Soviet Union or from the Soviet-bloc states. This situation, favorable for the maintenance of Albanian independence, was endangered by the improvement of relations between the Soviet Union and Yugoslavia after the death of Stalin. The possibility now threatened that Moscow might purchase Yugoslav support at Albania's expense. To gain other outside aid, Albania strengthened her ties with China. In 1956-57 Albania was able to win assistance from China as well as from the Soviet Union and the socialist bloc. Albanian relations with China grew in significance when a sharp ideological dispute broke out between Moscow and Peking in 1960.

More important, because of its wider implications, than the Yugoslav challenge to the Soviet Union was that offered by China. Again, what was in fact a struggle for political power was cloaked by ideological debate. Like Tito, the Chinese leaders now claimed to be purer in doctrine and better qualified to lead the socialist world. Khrushchev's policy of coexistence with the capitalist states and his failure to maintain a militant policy for the advance of Communism were attacked. China, now the champion of world revolution, also showed little fear of the consequences of atomic war. By 1960 it had become clear that China stood outside the Soviet camp; it was at this juncture that Albania spoke out in favor of the Chinese position. She immediately suffered from the same kind of pressure from the Soviet side that had previously been exerted upon Yugoslavia. Soviet economic aid was cut off and the Albanian regime was attacked by the radio and press of the socialist-bloc countries. At the Twenty-Second Party Congress in 1961, Khrushchev delivered a strong denunciation of Albania.

Both China and Albania now shared a similar attitude toward Yugoslavia. They both condemned its attempt to maintain a neutralist position and, unlike the Soviet Union, they refused even to recognize it as a socialist state. Peking thus provided support for Albania against Yugoslavia, but the distance and the relative poverty of

China meant that she could give little real aid. Through Albania, China now for the first time played an active, direct role in Balkan affairs. In her search for support, Albania turned also to the West, but not to the United States. Economic ties were again sought with Italy. In this difficult situation the poverty of Albania and her low standard of living were an asset because they made her less dependent on the outside world.

RUMANIA. The Sino-Soviet dispute and the defections of Yugoslavia and Albania from the Soviet bloc created the general conditions which allowed another state, Rumania, to alter its relations with its powerful neighbor. The source of the initial conflict was over the economic position which Rumania had been assigned in COMECON. This organization, set up in 1949 in answer to the Marshall Plan, was intended to promote economic cooperation and unity among the socialist states. Little was accomplished in the first years; each nation pursued its own goals and sought to build up its own economy. After 1956, under Soviet impetus, an attempt was made to introduce specialization and a division of labor among the member countries. This idea was advanced so far that in 1962, again with Soviet support, it was proposed that a supranational agency be created that would have authority to regulate and control the industry of the individual states. Until then, national independence had been guarded. Although the purely economic advantages of such a union were obvious, its dangerous political consequences were even more apparent. Most important for Rumania was the fact that the states with more highly developed industrial economies were to specialize in this direction. Thus Czechoslovakia and East Germany would have a favorable position. Rumania, in contrast, was to be primarily a source of raw materials, particularly grains and minerals. The plan would also have placed the socialist-bloc nations even more under Soviet influence because the Soviet Union would have retained not only her great military superiority but also her balanced economic system. The other states, in contrast, would have been inextricably linked to one another and to the Soviet Union.

At the time that the plan was proposed, Rumania was engaged in a great attempt to build up her own heavy industry, despite her lack of certain essential resources. Her success in this endeavor was particularly marked in the years 1960-62, when her industrial production increased by 55 per cent. The construction of an iron and steel complex at Galati was of major importance. The Rumanian government's opposition to COMECON was shown in its efforts to establish new trade relations, notably with the West, and its adoption of a more independent position toward Soviet leadership in the international field. In 1963, COMECON in effect accepted the Rumanian objections to a supranational controlling authority. In the same year, Rumania resumed her relations with Albania and also conducted negotiations with China and the West. In April 1964, in the strongest of the Rumanian declarations, the Rumanian Communist party asserted the equality of all Communist parties and again stated its position on COMECON.

It should be noted that this challenge to Soviet leadership within the socialist bloc was primarily national in direction. The Rumanian Communist party, although it did relax some internal controls after 1962, never deviated from its political goals. Like the Yugoslav and Albanian leaders, the Rumanians took their stand on general Marxist principles and argued the necessity of the construction of an industrial base for their socialist society. A position of conflict with the Soviet Union is extremely difficult for Rumania to maintain because of her long, exposed frontier and her relative military defenselessness before Moscow. Her situation is further complicated by her continuing bad relations with Hungary and the struggle over Transylvania. Bulgaria's close association with the Soviet Union also impedes Rumania's freedom of action.

BULGARIA. With the Rumanian challenge to COMECON and the attempt to set up new ties with the West, Bulgaria remained the single Balkan state which maintained its links with Moscow virtually unaltered since the end of the war. Czechoslovakia and East Germany were in a similar position. Nevertheless, Bulgaria also sought to improve its relations with its neighbors. Negotiations were carried on with Yugoslavia and a new highway has greatly facilitated communications between Belgrade and Sofia. In 1964, after several months of negotiation, Bulgaria reached an agreement with Greece on the questions of war reparations, communications between the two states, and territorial boundaries.

The postwar period in the Balkans thus brought about violent and radical changes. Not only was a new system of government introduced into four of the states, but these regimes brought about enormous alterations in the economic and social life of the countries in the area. Within a relatively short period, the diplomatic alignments of these states underwent a series of changes. In the years immediately after the war, it appeared that the great nightmare of the British in the nineteenth century, Russian domination of the Balkans, would indeed be realized in the twentieth. This event was hindered by the intervention of the United States in Greece and the refusal of Yugoslavia to follow Soviet dictation. The greatest challenge to Soviet Communist-world leadership, that offered by China, found approval in Albania. The American military and economic support given to Greece and Turkey and, later, to Yugoslavia also aided in limiting Soviet influence. Despite the re-establishment of this balance of forces, conditions within the Balkan states and also between them have not remained stable. The Greek conflict with Turkey over Cyprus and the attempts of Rumania to resist outside control over its economic life are only examples of the type of disputes and tensions which will undoubtedly continue in the future.

```
┌─────────────────────────────┐
│                             │
│           NINE              │
│                             │
│        CONCLUSION           │
│                             │
│                             │
│                             │
└─────────────────────────────┘
```

In the proceding pages, the conditions within the Balkan states today and the stages by which this development was attained have been discussed. In the years covered by this survey, three themes have recurred: the national sentiments of the Balkan peoples and the conflicts among them; the interference of the great powers in Balkan affairs; and the economic backwardness of the area compared with other sections of Europe.

Nationalism

Of the three, the influence of nationalism has certainly been the greatest. In the Middle Ages the Bulgarian, Byzantine, and Serbian states competed for the domination of the Balkan peninsula, and this basic rivalry is reflected in the present struggle over Macedonia. The medieval period also marked the foundation of national centers in the Danubian Principalities, Transylvania, and Croatia, as well as in Bosnia and Slovenia. The feeling of national individuality and uniqueness was not extinguished even during the fifteenth century, when the Balkan peninsula fell under Ottoman rule. Although the Ottoman government regarded all Christians as one body united through their religion, the Christian churches themselves remained divided. Because the churches also fulfilled the functions of civil government for the Christians under Ottoman rule, the ecclesiastical organizations became the transmitters and guardians of the national identity of the subject peoples. Thus the common Orthodox religion of the Bulgarians, the Serbs, and the Greeks led—not to cooperation among them—but to struggles over education, language, and ecclesiastical jurisdiction. The religious division in the Balkans was made all the more difficult by the fact that the Croats and Slovenes were Catholics. Like the national Orthodox churches, the Catholic Church too became a bulwark of nationalism.

The mutual antagonism that characterized the religious scene was also apparent during the struggles for national liberation. Despite the fact that all the Christian peoples had a common interest in throwing off Turkish control, they gave one another remarkably little assistance. Instead, each state turned to a great power for support and often fought the national aspirations of its neighbors. The conflict between the Greeks and the Rumanians was harmful to the national movements of both peoples. Greek hostility to the establishment of the Bulgarian exarchate, despite the fact that Greece had its own independent church, and Serbia's attack on Bulgaria in 1885, are other examples. More recently, the repeated attempts of Greece and Yugoslavia to encroach upon Albania and the willingness of all of the Balkan states to annex their neighbors' territories when the international situation allowed, shows the continuation of this lack of solidarity. The Balkan states have usually stood for the unique national rights of their own people, not necessarily for those of others. When the application of the concept of self-determination went against the interest of any state, that government was certain to shift the basis of the argument. Nationalism in the Balkans, as in the rest of Europe, thus led to the breakup of the old empires and to the formation of independent states, but it also resulted in the establishment of an almost constant state of tension among these new nations.

It has been shown how in their national development the Balkan governments took the political ideas of the West, modified them, and adapted them to their own needs. Western liberalism and, later, socialism formed the basis of the governments. It should also be noted that the emphasis on the attainment of national unity and, later, on economic reform has left little room for the development or the understanding of Western conceptions of personal freedom. In very few periods of Balkan history have any of the peoples enjoyed civil liberties in the American or British sense of the term. The word *freedom* in the Balkans has meant almost exclusively *national freedom*, not the right of the individual to dissent against the government or the majority opinion. The poverty, the low level or complete lack of general education, the history of constant war and national crisis, and outside political influences serve to explain this condition. Balkan politics resemble those of other areas in the world with similar economic and historical backgrounds.

External Interference

The political weakness of the Balkans invited outside intervention. The geographic position of the peninsula as the crossroads between Europe, Asia, and Africa, and the configuration of the land itself, made invasion relatively easy. Although the Balkan states were independent in ancient and medieval times, after the fifteenth century the entire region was usually either part of a non-Balkan state or in its sphere of influence.

Of first importance to the life of Balkan people was the almost five-hundred-year-long domination by the Ottoman Empire. During this period the area became a pawn in the European balance-of-power system. The great states of Europe used the Balkan nations and the Ottoman Empire to enhance their own strength and to thwart their opponents. It is interesting to note that, as the military power of the Ottoman Empire declined, its place in European diplomacy actually rose in importance. The governments of Europe could support Ottoman territorial integrity and attempt to dominate the central government; they could conquer Turkish territory and partition it among themselves; or they could support the liberation of the subject people. All these solutions were tried at one time or another.

The first state that sought to make an ally of the Ottoman Empire was France, which wished to use Ottoman power against the Habsburg Empire and, later, against Russia. In contrast, Austria and Russia sought to conquer and divide the empire. By the end of the eighteenth century, the Habsburg Empire had been able to acquire Hungary, Croatia, Slavonia, and Transylvania; at the same time, Russia reached the shores of the Black Sea and laid claim to a protectorship over the Balkan Christians. The French Revolution and the Napoleonic Wars caused a further shift in the diplomatic position of the nations. With the elimination of France as a danger to the European balance of power, Russia now appeared as the major threat. Britain and Austria thus joined to prevent a further extension of Russian control in the Balkans, and on most occasions they supported the maintenance of the Ottoman Empire. Russian policy itself was divided between the desire to conserve legitimate governments and the wish to continue the tradition of aid to Balkan Orthodoxy. Nevertheless, the first half of the nineteenth century witnessed the establishment of an independent Greece and the granting of autonomy to Serbia and the Danubian Principalities. A further crisis in the middle of the century led to the outbreak of the Crimean War. At this time Britain and France went to war with Russia in order to prevent what they feared was the possibility of predominant Russian control over the Balkans.

The attitude of Great Britain toward the preservation of the Ottoman Empire was maintained throughout the nineteenth century, although some consideration was given to the possibility that free states might indeed form a better barrier against Russian penetration. It was therefore with French and Russian support that the modern Rumanian state was established; another Russo-Turkish War gave the Bulgarians an autonomous government. The Balkan diplomatic scene again changed when a unified Germany and Italy entered into the imperial power struggles of Europe. World War I started over a Balkan incident brought about because of the national question in the Habsburg Empire.

When World War I ended in 1918, the entire balance of power in eastern Europe was again upset. Four empires—the Russian, the German, the Austro-Hungarian, and the Ottoman, all of which had played a major role in Balkan affairs—were either destroyed or temporarily eliminated from the diplomatic scene. Victorious France immediately stepped in to fill the vacuum thus created. She joined two of the Balkan states, Rumania and Yugoslavia, with Czechoslovakia in order to form the Little Entente, an alignment designed to act as a bulwark against Germany and Hungary. This alliance of the powers which were satisfied with the outcome of the war led to the formation of a counteralliance, under Italian leadership, of those who wished to change the peace settlements. The rise of Nazi Germany in the 1930s ended this balance of power between opposing camps and again the Balkans faced the threat of domination by a single power. For a period during World War II, German forces were in control of the entire peninsula.

The elimination of Germany and Italy by their defeat in the war left the Soviet Union as the greatest military power in eastern Europe. To prevent the entire area from coming under Soviet control, the United States undertook the role played by Britain in the nineteenth century and attempted to contain Soviet influence. Thereafter American military and economic aid, together with China's challenge to the Soviet Union, created a situation in which the Balkan states were able to gain more freedom of action. Although a balance of power has again been re-established, the situation is not stable. A shift in the relationship of the great powers could once again bring about a realignment of the Balkan states.

Since the actions of the non-Balkan powers have always quite obviously and naturally been dictated by their own national interests, a question arises: Why do the Balkan people not cooperate with one another and resist foreign interference? They are united in many ways. They have a similar history and a common Balkan character. The Albanians, the Bulgarians, the Greeks, the Serbs, and the Rumanians are Orthodox; the Yugoslavs and the Bulgarians have very similar languages. They all suffer from the consequences of foreign control and economic backwardness. Nevertheless, despite these points of unity, the possibility of achieving effective cooperation among the Balkan nations has always been—and still is—even more remote than the securing of similar relations among the states of western Europe. Although there were plans for a Balkan union in the nineteenth century and further efforts in this direction in the 1930s, all these attempts went down to defeat before the forces of competitive nationalism.

The situation today is particularly interesting. In theory, Communism calls for the union of the working people of the world without national distinctions. In practice, the socialist nations of the world are more divided among themselves than are their capitalist counterparts. During and after the war, each Communist party, with the exception of the Albanian, developed on its own; there was comparatively little cooperation with similar groups in neighboring Balkan states. In fact, the stronger the Communist party, the more nationalistic and independent was its attitude. Moreover, although the Soviet Union is the leader of the Soviet-bloc states of Europe in both a political and an ideological sense, she—like all states in a similar position in the past—has an interest in keeping her weaker allies divided among themselves and dependent upon her. The policy of "divide and rule" is clearly to her benefit as a great power and conforms to diplomatic tradition. Therefore, despite a common socialist ideology among four of the states, the Balkan governments remain as divided as ever.

Economic Backwardness

The third problem, the necessity of raising the standard of life in the Balkans, is of particular importance today. The Balkan peninsula, considered as a whole, is the most economically backward section of Europe, and stands between western Europe and the colonial areas in general economic development. This condition is the result of its long history of domination by a power that was itself in a state of decline and of the effects of centuries of war and internal crisis. The Ottoman Empire not only did not develop the lands under its control, it also left a legacy of maladministration and corruption in public life that influenced and burdened the new governments. The necessity of radically changing the economic conditions in the Balkans is both a question of the improvement of standards and of survival. The rising birth rates in all the Balkan states and the pressure of outside events have already necessitated radical alterations in all the countries, whether they be socialistic or capitalistic.

In fact, it is in the economic section of national life that the most marked improvement has been accomplished since World War II. The problem has been recognized and attempts are being made to meet it. The industrial development of the Balkan states has quite obviously improved the material conditions of life although the nations still lag much behind the west. Most important has been the development of transportation—particularly the extension of the road network and the availability of air transport throughout the Balkans. This steady rise should continue in the future in all of the states.

It is difficult to generalize upon the present events in the Balkans or to attempt to foretell probable future changes there. Today, as in the past, conditions in the Balkans are tied to world events. Decisions taken in Moscow and Washington—and also in Peking, Paris, Bonn, Rome, and London—will set the pattern for Balkan developments. The area is today, as it has so often been in the past, a battlefield for contending ideas and power groups. Thus any conflict between the great international blocs is bound to have an effect within the Balkan peninsula. The fascination of the area has always lain in the contradictions and conflicts of its history, but the very conditions which appear romantic or exciting to the student or the casual observer are those which have made unusually difficult the lives of the people directly involved. Unfortunately, because the strategic significance of the Balkan peninsula cannot be altered and because the conflict between the great power blocs does not seem close to resolution, the national life of the area will probably follow much the same path it has in the past. The Balkans will remain a crossroads where competing systems meet, an area of danger and conflict.

General Reading

The standard survey of Balkan history is Leften S. Stavrianos, *The Balkans since 1453* (New York: Holt, Rinehart & Winston, Inc., 1958). The author presents the main events and trends from the fall of Constantinople to the end of World War II. His book shows a keen appreciation and feeling for Balkan affairs. It also contains a seventy-five-page critically annotated bibliography of the major works in all languages, which should be consulted by anyone seriously interested in Balkan studies. Various aspects of Balkan problems since the eighteenth century are carefully analyzed by outstanding scholars in thirteen essays in Charles and Barbara Jelavich (eds.), *The Balkans in Transition: Essays in the Development of Balkan Life and Politics since the Eighteenth Century* (Berkeley: University of California Press, 1963). The general developments from 1941 to 1955, especially the Communist seizure and consolidation of power, are ably interpreted by Robert Lee Wolff, *The Balkans in Our Times* (Cambridge, Mass.: Harvard University Press, 1956).

Although ancient Greece is not within the scope of this survey, a brief comment has been made on the Byzantine background of Balkan history. Two of the best general works are by Georgije Ostrogorsky, *History of the Byzantine State* (New Brunswick, N.J.: Rutgers University Press, 1957) and A. A. Vasiliev, *History of the Byzantine Empire* (Madison: University of Wisconsin Press, 1961), 2 vols. The role of the Balkan peoples in Slavic history is presented with understanding and great erudition by one of the great Byzantinists, Francis Dvornik, in *The Slavs in European History and Civilization* (New Brunswick, N.J.: Rutgers University Press, 1962).

For almost five centuries the history of the Balkan Peninsula was inseparably bound with that of the Ottoman Empire. Unfortunately, there is as yet no good history of the Ottoman Turks in English. The well-known work by Sir Charles Eliot, *Turkey in Europe* (London: Edward Arnold, Publishers, Ltd., 1908) is good, but outdated. The recent volume by Bernard Lewis, *The Emergence of Modern Turkey* (London: Oxford University Press, 1961), centers on the nineteenth and twentieth centuries. There are, however, monographs which concentrate on certain developments. The reign of Suleiman the Magnificent is presented in the pioneer work by Albert Howe Lybyer, *The Government of the Ottoman Empire in the Time of Suleiman the Magnificent* (Cambridge, Mass.: Harvard University Press, 1913). The crucial period of the eighteenth century is thoroughly analyzed in the major work by H. A. R. Gibb and H. Bowen, *Islamic Society and the West: A Study of the Impact of Western Civilization on Moslem Culture in the Near East* (London: Oxford University Press, 1950, 1960), 1 vol., 2 parts. This book should be supplemented by the valuable economic study for the eighteenth and nineteenth centuries by Traian Stoianovich, "The Conquering Balkan Orthodox Merchant," *Journal of Economic History*, XX:2 (June 1960), 234-313. The reform measures of the nineteenth century have received much attention. Among the valuable works on the subject are F. E. Bailey, *British Policy and the Turkish Reform Movement: A Study in Anglo-Turkish Relations 1826-1853* (Cambridge, Mass.: Harvard University Press, 1942); R. H. Davison, *Reform in the Ottoman Empire, 1856-1876* (Princeton, N.J.: Princeton University Press, 1963); and Robert Devereux, *The First Ottoman Constitutional Period: A Study of the Midhat Constitution and Parliament* (Baltimore: John Hopkins Press, 1963). Two good books on Turkish intellectual developments are: Serif Mardin, *The Genesis of Young Ottoman Thought: A Study in the Modernization of Turkish Political Ideas* (Princeton, N.J.: Princeton University Press, 1962), and E. E. Ramsauer, *The Young Turks: Prelude to the Revolution of 1908* (Princeton, N.J.: University Press, 1957).

The economic and financial aspects of some of the problems of the Ottoman Empire are considered in D. C. Blaisdell, *European Financial Control in the Ottoman Empire: A Study of the Establishment, Activities, and Significance of the Administration of the Ottoman Public Debt* (New

York: Columbia University Press, 1929), and Herbert Feis, *Europe the World's Banker, 1870-1914* (New York: A. M. Kelley, 1961).

Individual Countries

There is no good general history of Yugoslavia in English. Two older works, one by the father of modern historical scholarship, Leopold von Ranke, *A History of Servia and the Servian Revolution* (London: Bohn, 1853) and H. W. V. Temperley, *History of Serbia* (London: G. Bell & Sons, Ltd., 1917), still may be examined with profit. An excellent economic history of the South Slavs does, however, exist: Jozo Tomasevich, *Peasants, Politics, and Economic Change in Jugoslavia* (Stanford: Stanford University Press, 1955). A valuable supplement to the latter is Peter F. Sugar, *Industrialization of Bosnia-Hercegovina, 1878-1918* (Seattle: University of Washington Press, 1964). The first manifestations of socialism in the Balkans are discussed in Woodford D. McClellan, *Svetozar Marković and the Origins of Balkan Socialism* (Princeton, N.J.: Princeton University Press, 1964). The diplomatic position of Serbia is examined in Wayne S. Vucinich, *Serbia between East and West: the Events of 1903-1908* (Stanford: Stanford University Press, 1954). Perhaps the best work in English on the Croats is still R. W. Seton-Watson, *The Southern Slav Question and the Habsburg Monarchy* (London: Constable & Son, Ltd., 1911). For recent Yugoslav history the essays in Robert F. Byrnes (ed.), *Yugoslavia* (New York: Mid-European Studies Center, 1957), are informative.

There is no satisfactory history of modern Greece in English, although there are more books on this country than on any other in the Balkans. The study of the distinguished Philhellene, George Finlay, *A History of Greece from its Conquest by the Romans to the Present Time, 146 B.C. to 1864 A.D.* (Oxford: Clarendon Press, 1877), 7 vols., is still worth consulting, especially Vol. VI and VII. Two good general surveys are William Miller, *A History of the Greek People, 1821-1921* (London: Methuen & Co., Ltd., 1922), and E. S. Forster, *A Short History of Modern Greece, 1821-1956*, 3rd. ed., revised by Douglas Dakin (London: Methuen & Co., Ltd., 1958).

Because the Greek revolution played such an important role in European diplomacy during the era of Metternich, there are quite a number of books on this subject. To be particularly recommended are Christopher M. Woodhouse, *The Greek War of Independence: Its Historical Setting* (London: Hutchinson & Co. [Publishers], Ltd., 1952); C. W. Crawley, *The Question of Greek Independence: A Study of British Policy in the*

Near East, 1821-1833 (Cambridge: Cambridge University Press, 1930), and Douglas Dakin, *British and American Philhellenes during the War of Greek Independence, 1821-1833* (Thessaloniki: Institute for Balkan Studies, 1955). The most influential of modern Greek statesmen was E. Venizelos. Although a definitive biography is yet to be written, Doros Alastos, *Venizelos: Patriot, Statesman, Revolutionary* (London: P. Lund, Humphries, & Co., 1942), may be consulted with profit.

Unlike the other Balkan states, Rumania does have a good scholarly study of its history: R. W. Seton-Watson, *A History of the Rumanians from Roman Times to the Completion of Unity* (Cambridge: Cambridge University Press, 1934). The Rumanian national movement is discussed by John C. Campbell, "French Influence and the Rise of Rumanian Nationalism," an unpublished doctoral dissertation presented at Harvard University, Cambridge, Mass., 1940. The unification of the country is presented with great skill by T. W. Riker, *The Making of Rumania: A Study of an International Problem, 1856-1866* (Oxford: Oxford University Press, 1941). Russia's role in the unification is analyzed in Barbara Jelavich, *Russia and the Rumanian National Cause, 1858-1859* (Bloomington: Indiana University Press, 1959). Two excellent studies of Rumanian agrarian conditions are D. Mitrany, *The Land and the Peasant in Rumania: The War and Agrarian Reform* (1917-1921) (London: Oxford University Press, 1930), and Henry L. Roberts, *Rumania: Political Problems of an Agrarian State* (New Haven: Yale University Press, 1951), which covers the modern period. Stephen A. Fischer-Galati (ed.), *Romania* (New York: Mid-European Studies Center, 1957), contains important essays on recent developments.

The two states which have received the least study are Bulgaria and Albania. The recent work by Mercia Macdermott, *A History of Bulgaria, 1393-1885* (London: George Allen & Unwin, 1962), is sympathetic with current Bulgarian writing. George C. Logio, *Bulgaria Past and Present* (Manchester: Sheratt and Hughes, 1936), is usable but sketchy. L. A. D. Dellin (ed.), *Bulgaria* (New York: Mid-European Studies Center, 1957), includes essays on contemporary problems. The formation of the Bulgarian state is examined in C. E. Black, *The Establishment of Constitutional Government in Bulgaria* (Princeton, N.J.: Princeton University Press, 1943), and Charles Jelavich, *Tsarist Russia and Balkan Nationalism: Russian Influence in the Internal Affairs of Bulgaria and Serbia, 1876-1886* (Berkeley: University of California Press, 1958).

Stavro Skendi (ed.), *Albania* (New York: Mid-European Studies Center, 1956), is the best introduction to this state. An older work of interest is Joseph Swire, *Albania: the Rise of a Kingdom* (London: Williams and Ungate, 1929).

Specific Issues

Because the peasant has been and still is the backbone of Balkan life, it is understandable that he should be the center of valuable studies. One should consult, on this subject, two books by Irwin T. Sanders: *Balkan Village* (Lexington: University of Kentucky Press, 1949), which centers on a Bulgarian village, and *Rainbow in the Rock: the People of Rural Greece* (Cambridge, Mass.: Harvard University Press, 1961), a similar study of Greece. Another excellent book on Greek village life is Ernestine Friedl, *Vasilika: A Village in Modern Greece* (New York: Holt, Rinehart & Winston, Inc., 1962). A case study of a South Slav village is in Joel M. Halpern, *A Serbian Village* (New York: Columbia University Press, 1958).

Much of the diplomatic history of the nineteenth century centers on the Balkan peninsula and the problems caused by the decline of the Ottoman Empire. A general survey of the entire problem is to be found in J. A. R. Marriott, *The Eastern Question* (Oxford: Clarendon Press, 1951). The Russian position can be found in Barbara Jelavich, *A Century of Russian Foreign Policy, 1814-1914* (Philadelphia: J. B. Lippincott Co., 1964), and in Ivo Lederer (ed.), *Russian Foreign Policy: Essays in Historical Perspective* (New Haven: Yale University Press, 1962). The latter volume is made up of nineteen essays by scholars in the Russian field who discuss the question of continuity between tsarist and Soviet foreign policies. There are many special studies on individual events. The problem of the control of the eastern Mediterranean is discussed in Philip E. Mosely, *Russian Diplomacy and the Opening of the Eastern Question in 1838 and 1839* (Cambridge, Mass.: Harvard University Press, 1934). The Crimean War is described in H. W. V. Temperley, *England and the Near East: the Crimea* (London: Longmans, Green & Company, Ltd., 1936), which also covers the first Turkish reforms, and Vernon J. Puryear, *England, Russia, and the Straits Question, 1844-1856* (Berkeley: University of California Press, 1931). Panslavism, which had a great influence on the relations of Russia and the Balkan Slavs after the Crimean War, is analyzed in Michael Boro Petrovich, *The Emergence of Russian Panslavism, 1856-1870* (New York: Columbia University Press, 1956). Many able studies have been made of the events surrounding the Bosnian Crisis of 1875-78 and the Congress of Berlin. Two of the most comprehensive treatments are B. H. Sumner, *Russia and the Balkans, 1870-1880*

(Oxford: Oxford University Press, 1937), and William L. Langer, *European Alliances and Alignments, 1871-1890*, 2nd. ed. (New York: Alfred A. Knopf, Inc., 1956).

The Macedonian problem has produced few scholarly works, but there are many partisan tracts. Perhaps the best introduction to the issue is a careful study by Henry R. Wilkinson, *Maps and Politics: A Review of the Ethnographic Cartography of Macedonia* (Liverpool: University Press, 1951), which shows how the contending sides used maps to bolster their arguments. Other books to be recommended are Leften S. Stavrianos, *Balkan Federation: A History of the Movement Toward Balkan Unity in Modern Times* (Northampton, Mass.: Smith College, 1944), which shows how the Macedonian quarrel prevented Balkan unity, and Elizabeth Barker, *Macedonia: Its Place in Balkan Power Politics* (London: Royal Institute of International Affairs, 1950), which also discusses present conditions.

The two crises immediately preceding the outbreak of the war in 1914 are discussed in Bernadotte E. Schmitt, *The Annexation of Bosnia, 1908-1909* (Cambridge: Cambridge University Press, 1937), and Ernst C. Helmreich, *The Diplomacy of the Balkan Wars, 1912-1913* (Cambridge, Mass.: Harvard University Press, 1938). Of the many books dealing with the origins of World War I, a more recent scholarly contribution is Luigi Albertini, *The Origins of the War of 1914* (London: Oxford University Press, 1952-57), 3 vols. An account of the assassination of Franz Ferdinand is in Joachim Remak, *Sarajevo: The Story of a Political Murder* (New York: Criterion Press, 1959).

The territorial and political changes in the Balkans after the war have been dealt with in a series of able monographs. The role of the United States is described in Victor S. Mamatey, *The United States and East Central Europe 1914-1918: A Study in Wilsonian Diplomacy and Propaganda* (Princeton, N.J.: Princeton University Press, 1957). The breakup of the Ottoman Empire is covered in Harry N. Howard, *The Partition of Turkey: A Diplomatic History 1913-1923* (Norman: Oklahoma University Press, 1931). The problems of the new South Slav State are analyzed in Ivo J. Lederer, *Yugoslavia at the Paris Peace Conference: A Study in Frontier-Making* (New Haven: Yale University Press, 1963). A similar study for Rumania is Sherman David Spector, *Rumania at the Paris Peace Conference: A Study of the Diplomacy of Ioan I. C. Bratianu* (New York: Bookman Associates, 1962). The Greek and Bulgarian settlements can be found in A. A. Pallis, *Greece's Anatolian Venture and After* (London: Hutchinson & Co. [Publishers], Ltd., 1937), and Georgi P.

Genov, *Bulgaria and the Treaty of Neuilly* (Sofia: H. G. Danov & Co., 1935).

The important interwar period, unfortunately, has been largely neglected until now. The two best surveys are Hugh Seton-Watson, *Eastern Europe between the Wars, 1918-1941*, 3rd. ed. (Hamden, Conn.: Archon, 1962), and C. A. Macartney and A. W. Palmer, *Independent Eastern Europe: A History* (London: Macmillan & Co., Ltd., 1962). For Yugoslavia and Rumania, the excellent books by Tomasevich and Roberts which have already been cited should be consulted. The years from the assassination of King Alexander to Hitler's assault on Yugoslavia is examined by Jacob B. Hoptner, *Yugoslavia in Crisis, 1934-1941* (New York: Columbia University Press, 1962). Bulgarian developments are described in Joseph Rothschild, *The Communist Party of Bulgaria: Origins and Development, 1883-1936* (New York: Columbia University Press, 1959).

In contrast, World War II and the subsequent political changes have been discussed in numerous publications. Two of the best general surveys are the volume by Wolff cited previously and Hugh Seton-Watson, *The East European Revolution*, 3rd. ed. (New York: Frederick A. Praeger, Inc., 1961). The economic changes brought about under the new regimes are discussed in Nicolas Spulber, *The Economics of Communist Eastern Europe* (Cambridge, Mass.: M.I.T. Press, 1957) and Irwin T. Sanders (ed.), *Collectivization of Agriculture in Eastern Europe* (Lexington: University of Kentucky Press, 1959). The study of Richard V. Burks, *The Dynamics of Communism in Eastern Europe* (Princeton, N.J.: Princeton University Press, 1961), assesses the strength of Communist power and its success. Among the more recent discussions of the Soviet bloc as a whole are Zbigniew K. Brzezinski, *The Soviet Bloc: Unity and Conflict*, rev. ed. (New York: Frederick A. Praeger, Inc., 1962); Stephen Fischer-Galati (ed.), *Eastern Europe in the Sixties* (New York: Frederick A. Praeger, Inc., 1963); Leopold Labedz (ed.), *Revisionism* (New York: Frederick A. Praeger, Inc., 1962); and Walter Laqueur and Leopold Labedz, *Polycentrism* (New York: Frederick A. Praeger, Inc., 1962).

Of the individual events of the postwar period, the question of Yugoslavia has received the most attention. Among the best studies of the break between Tito and Stalin are Hamilton Fish Armstrong, *Tito and Goliath* (New York. The Macmillan Company, 1951), and Adam Ulam, *Titoism and the Cominform* (Cambridge, Mass.: Harvard University Press, 1952). A recent excellent account of present developments is George W. Hoffman and Fred Warner Neal, *Yugoslavia and the New Communism* (New York: Twentieth Century Fund, 1962). A critical analysis is Alex N. Dragnich, *Tito's Promised Land: Yugoslavia* (New Brunswick, N.J.: Rutgers University Press, 1954). Milovan Djilas, *The New Class: An Analysis of the Communist System* (New York: Frederick A. Praeger, Inc., 1957), reveals the disillusionment of Tito's onetime close associate.

The Greek civil war has also been carefully studied. Among the books concerning this development are William H. McNeill, *The Greek Dilemma: War and Aftermath* (Philadelphia: J. B. Lippincott Co., 1947); Leften S. Stavrianos, *Greece: American Dilemma and Opportunity* (Chicago: Henry Regnery Co., 1952), and Bickham Sweet-Escott, *Greece: A Political and Economic Survey, 1939-1953* (London: Royal Institute of International Affairs, 1954). The diplomatic background is presented in Stephen G. Xydis, *Greece and the Great Powers, 1944–1947: Prelude to the Truman Doctrine* (Thessaloniki: Institute for Balkan Studies, 1963). The more recent Albanian crisis and its relation to the larger Sino-Soviet dispute is investigated in William E. Griffith, *Albania and the Sino-Soviet Rift* (Cambridge, Mass.: M.I.T. Press, 1963).

The reader is also referred to three recent paperback surveys by Balkan specialists: George W. Hoffman, *The Balkans in Transition* (New York: D. Van Nostrand Co., Inc., 1963); Joseph Rothchild, *Communist Eastern Europe* (New York: Walker & Company, 1964), and Leften S. Stavrianos, *The Balkans, 1815-1914* (New York: Holt, Rinehart & Winston, Inc., 1963).

In the field of Balkan literature, the works of the Yugoslav Nobel Prize winner, Ivo Andrić, are strongly recommended, in particular, *Bosnian Story* (London: Lincolns-Praeger, 1948), and *The Bridge on the Drina* (New York: New American Library, 1961). Of equal value for Greek conditions are the novels of Nikos Kazantzakis, especially, *Freedom or Death* (New York: Simon & Schuster, Inc., 1961), *The Greek Passion* (New York: Simon & Schuster, Inc., 1959), and *Zorba the Greek* (New York: Simon & Schuster, Inc., 1952). Life in Rumania in the nineteenth century is portrayed in Petru Dumitriu, *Family Jewels* (New York: Pantheon Books, Inc., 1961). Ivan Minchov Vazov, *Under the Yoke* (Sofia: Foreign Languages Press, 1960) deals with Bulgaria under Ottoman rule.

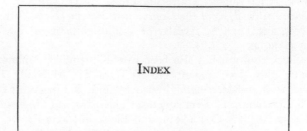

INDEX